THE TEST

THE TEST

if there was no Sex,
how would the relationship
between guys and girls change?

LUCA GRISENDI

THE TEST
IF THERE WAS NO SEX, HOW WOULD THE RELATIONSHIP BETWEEN GUYS AND GIRLS CHANGE?

ISBN: 978-1-4917-6077-2 (sc)
ISBN: 978-1-4917-6078-9 (e)

Print information available on the last page.

iUniverse rev. date: 02/18/2015

Contact: Luca Grisendi

sedicesimi@yahoo.it

www.LucaGrisendiArt.com

To my family

To my family

The author:

Hello, my name is Luke. Honestly, I never thought of writing a book. At school I wasn't a nerd and some Italian was not my favorite subject. At that time I had many other things on my mind, as I think a bit 'all the boys and girls attending high school. However, over time I've heard instilled in me the need to express what was inside. The result is a book that I think is original in its kind.

The initial question ("How would the relationship between guys and girls change if there were no sex?") Is a provocation to which I have tried to answer through the story told below. What happens to the protagonist Luke and his friends is far from obvious, as you have the opportunity to read. I wrote this book because I want the experiences narrated in the story can actually materialize in my life. In the end it would be nice if you could put on paper what you want and after a short time, get it?

My site: www.LucaGrisendi.com
I am not only a writer but also:
A Personal Trainer: www.LucaGrisendiPersonalTrainer.com
A drummer and music producer: www.LucaGrisendiArt.com

Abstract:

Not satisfied with their relational situation with girls, the guys form a high school lead by Luke decide to start an audacious Test inside their high school in order to answer the question: "If there was now sex, how would the relationship between guys and girls change?" For the entire period of 30 days, all guys from the high school will radically change their attitude creating the craziest experiment ever seen before in a high school!

Trough difficulties, pleasure, fun moments and personal growth, Luke and his friends will finally discover the taste of payback.

Started as a pure provocation and action of bravery, the Test pushes the guys to face their own fears and their deep desires, making them realize that their real potential lies inside themselves, waiting to boom. The process becomes a source of pure inspiration and pleasure, offering new life to the main character Luke and to his fellows after having their lives consciously in their hands. Teens of the guys is not only superficial but also a journey heading to a new self consciousness and new way of life where the word limit becomes senseless. At this point girls become an inspiration for Luke to fuel his personal change which he needed for so long. Each day turns out as a rich search of breath-taking adventures before it's too late and regret prevails. The end will be another shocking starting point that will challenge the main character Luke over again.

Contents

CHAPTER 1

THE EVENING WHEN
THE WHOLE THING STARTED

Thursday, September the 15ᵗʰ

"Luke! Luke, come on move!" I heard the voice echoing in the stairwell while I was running to the living room. Summer was ending and I felt the cool air blowing from the open window that anticipated autumn. I got into the living room breathless, after completing an entire flight of stairs in a record time. I was dating Giulia at that time, a girl who made me crazy and I used to spend whole afternoons with her. John, my best friend, was calling me after getting into my house while I didn't even heard the doorbell ring. I ran to him in shorts and flip-flops. We arranged to go out together that evening and he was there before the scheduled time. "Come on hurry up! 'Something important to tell you!"

"Coming, coming...chill out, dude!" I went upstairs again and immediately got dressed intrigued by what John had to say. After all, he was a very predictable guy and if he had something to tell me, it was definitely something tasty. "Where are you going?" Asked Giulia.

"'I'm going out with John, going for a drink. Do you want me to drive you home?" "Ya better, otherwise I have to ask my father."

Giulia was still without a driving license and her father and me were the only means of transport she could count on. I drove her home while John, that's what he told me, was already going to the pub where some of our friends were waiting for us. My curiosity was getting bigger and bigger: it seemed that he had gathered at least 6 people: what was going on? I got to

1

the pub and joined the gang at the table. They already ordered their beer; I had a Guinness and sat impatiently; I really wanted to hear what John had to tell us. "Are you still dating Valentina?" One of the guys asked John.

"Yeah .. now let Luke explain his idea." I found myself completely unprepared: "What idea John?" The fact that John didn't tell me anything made everything even more mysterious. John immediately told me: "What you told me about last night...your crazy but brilliant. idea." Immediately came to mind what he meant: "Oh yeah! Haha. "Meanwhile all these guys really seemed not to understand what was happening. So I started my speech: "What I'm about to say may sound a bit strange at first but please let me finish my speech. In the last weeks I have been thinking over our recent experiences and I felt the need to share all this with you all. As you know, the relationship between sexes is not easy and often misunderstandings are daily stuff. Every single weekend we try to meet some chicks but, as we well know, we keep going home every time without concluding anything.

"No doubt about it! You're right, dude!" John's friend claimed.

"You got it, my friend!" I said and continued: "We often wonder why it is so difficult to even chit-chat with a girl, plus we never get to anything and we don't even know the reason why. I know we all feel deep inside to deserve more and that the current situation does not reflect our true potential. It can happen, in best cases, we can get the girl's cell number or facebook contact but no one goes very much further. So I thought it is time to change the approach completely. The girls expect us to make the first move and they have so many opportunities that put them in the position to choose. But all this thanks to us. What if we stopped hooking them up for a while? How would the power balance change? In other words: "If there was no sex, how would the relationship between guys and girls change?" The audience fell in deep silence, interrupted by a friend of John: "Abstinence is hard!" A big laughter filled the air.

I kept going on impassive, reiterating the idea: "The girls are always waiting for the guys to make the first move and are accustomed to receiving more avanches. So they have the possibility to choose who to go out with and show the bitch shield if they feel like it. They are therefore in a stronger position towards us because we always have to struggle to achieve each result. The point then is to change, for a month, these consolidated habits: it will be a real revolution that will mess up the status quo!". I, after all, raised a problem that was well known to us, whether we wanted to recognize it or not. The relationship between sexes was always complicated because of incompatible differences in the way guys and girls relate to each other. But this issue represented an important question that could also help us find more satisfactory answers. I continued. "After this initial consideration, this is my idea: for a period of one month we'll quit to dedicate all our attentions to girls as we usually do. We won't chase after chicks anymore and we will act simply as friends." A moment of silence fell in the air. John was confused and did not know what to say. It was clear that chasing after girls didn't give us satisfactory results and one month was not that long. Also, it could have been an interesting experiment. However, I immediately thought that in order to be effective, it was necessary that all the guys in our school joined.

Simon broke the silence asking: "Are you telling me that we have to stop talking with girls for one month? "No, no...absolutely. We will keep talking to them, but only as friends, without any further purpose." Simon then pressed me again: "What do you wish to prove trough this Test?" I was ready for this:"I honestly do not know exactly what will happen. I just think it's time to radically change our way to approach girls. We owe this to ourselves, to our potential. We all know we deserve more and if we keep acting the same things over and over, there will be no improvements, of course. If we break this chain in which girls always expect us to do the first move, we will definitely have a few more things to meditate on." John came with a spontaneous question: "How do you think girls will react?" I answered: "I do not know...I just know that they'll be shocked. But this will stop this negative series of failures. In fact, I feel that we are launching an unique experiment." Then I added: "In addition, girls know at some unconscious level that our approach to them is always driven by a strong sex urge. They expect it and they take it for granted. But if we scatter this illusion, for the duration of the Test, and show total indifference, this could only be an important shock and a good answer to our questions. They will perceive us as not interested in them, and this will make them go crazy. Imagine a beautiful girl, in school or in the club, not receiving any boy's advances..." The idea was definitely daring and courageous and I admired John for having the guts to organize this "meeting" with all of our friends.

Not to mention that I had just now realized that I had shared my crazy idea without hesitation with everyone. Our school counted more than 1,000 students and could certainly represent a good sample for our experiment. We still had to interview the other guys and ask their opinion. John and I had a good reputation at school and we were very popular so I thought it all could work. The freshmen would not have not been a problem: the only ones to convince would have been the guys of our age.

I then added: "My belief is that by stopping this ineffective and dysfunctional behavior, we can get some answers that will help us to improve..."

The only problem was, that no matter how popular we were, such a proposal could make us look like fools. All together we thought, however, that it was worth it. Maybe after a month we would have had more useful answers. We were at the beginning of the school year and even if this experiment didn't work out, we would have had time to go back to the old method before the school end: ask girls out, as usual. That evening the atmosphere was particular; each one of us agreed on something that kept inside for a long time and only I had the courage to share. After mine speech, a hot debate followed and lasted till late. It was six of us that night but we thought that our first group represented the beginning of something that would have involved all the guys in our school. At one o'clock we closed the debate and we went back home with so many thoughts bouncing in our heads. It was the last year of high school, just at the beginning of what would have been the last days as teenagers.

September was about to end and autumn was beginning. The sky that night seemed made of several clouds' coiled balls and fresh air pointed out to us that the summer was over. The time for summer parties and days at the pool were over and it was time to get ready for the last year that seemed to be quite interesting. I got home still with a thousand thoughts in my head. My cat Manuel welcomed me and seemed so happy to see me. I could not help myself thinking how much easier it was for him. His relationship with pussycats was certainly more intelligible and clear than our with girls. I gave him his usual meal that smelled pretty good and finally went to bed. I could not free my mind and fell asleep very late.

CHAPTER 2

ARE WE REALLY SURE
WE WANNA DO THIS?

Friday, September the 16th

The next morning the wake up was pretty hard. In the first hour we had Philosophy test. The professor was smart and could get our interest in his subject. The test was pretty simple and, from one thought to another on the evening before, we got to morning break.

"Luke, Luke, come here!" John's voice was already familiar to me.

In the courtyard John had gathered the guys of the night before, and the debate was animated. After the previous evening's discussion and the night's thoughts, we all had many doubts. Among John's friends, the witty Simon stood out. Today he was more doubtful and serious. He began saying, "You know Luke, I thought about it...surely the question you have raised is interesting but I honestly think that setting up this experiment is totally crazy!"

Simon's doubt was the same I had the night before and still in the morning. The idea was interesting but maybe it was too risky to go around the school and involve other guys. We did not know how they would react and certainly we did not want the other guys to look at us as a bunch of fools and to seem desperate to the girls. This was the last year of our high school adventure and we didn't want to lose the great popularity gained in five years. I then said to Simon: "I know this is something very different and we do not want to take this outside the school. I think if we start talking with some of the guy of our grade, we can start seeing the first reactions. If we carry on the Test till the end of the month, we will have many more answers and..." Simon interrupted me: "Or maybe the girls will just perceive us as losers and we won't have no more chances with no girl."

After Simon's intervention a nod of approval started among the other guys. At this age, what other people think of you is very important, and even if you're popular, the risk of looking stupid is so damn easy. Even more if you are involved in some weird experiments. "Guys, guys calm down! I know that what I have proposed is kind of weird but just stop for a minute and think: for how long we want to go on like this? Every weekend the same old story, a lot of effort but poor results with girls. With this experiment we could have some more information and anyway we're organizing things not to waste our credibility."

"What? How can we do that?" Simon asked. John kept pretty quiet but Simon was raising common doubts that reflected, I guess, what everyone thought. "First of all, we start showing the idea to the guys of our age to see their reaction. After that, if the answer is positive we begin to make it circulate around. If the initial response is good, we can go for it in the whole school. When the first guys will join the project, the rest will follow, especially if we involve the most popular ones at the beginning!" Simon seemed almost convinced and the same with John. The other guys seemed to follow the general mood. Definitely the thrill deriving from this kind of experiment was strong and so was the worry to look desperate. A Test of this kind had never been done and we really did not know what it could have happened.

The bell brought us back to the harsh reality: it was time to go back to class.

John and I walked together to the 5°G and Simon with the other guys went to the second floor, class 5°N. The conversation that had just ended had been probably the deepest we have ever had. We used to have light talks about girls. Today it seemed that maturity had arrived a little in advance! Back in class, we had the last 2 hours of lessons and then we were finally free. We spent the rest of the morning texting each other on WhatsApp and chatting on Facebook with other students of the school beginning to expand the working group. The seats in the last line in the class which John and I chose the first day of the school year came up as a great choice. After our first messages, we got the first responses from the guys of our age. We agreed with them to see us late in the morning in the courtyard, to talk about all the details. At 12:25 am, finally, the bell rang and happy with our newfound freedom, we got running into the yard where we found Robert and Jack, representatives of the school, waiting for us.

"I did not get anything of the message you wrote, Luke." Robert said, eager for answers. "Gosh, tough start!" I immediately thought. But it was normal: a weird idea like this could not be explained simply and completely by a message.

The crowd of students coming out of school was thinning, and we, despite the hunger that gripped us, stayed to go deeper. "Let me tell you..." I said.

"We want to set up an experiment within our school in order to have an answer to this question: If there was no sex, and all the consequences in terms of attention that we devote to girls, how would the relationship between us and them change? The relationship with girls is often not easy and even the guys who are more successful, complain knowing how easier things would be if the balance changed. If there was no sex, would we spend all this time and energy for girls? How would the relationship change?" Both Robert and Jack gasped. They certainly did not expect anything like this. I took the opportunity to continue: "For a period of one month, we will quit approaching girls with further drives, talking to them as if they were just friends without all the "concerned" attention that we usually give them. For a whole month, just with girls who attend our school, we will act as if sex did not exist. Only friendship, let's see what happens! This way we will take them the power that allows them to choose which guy to go out with, how, where and when. We are the ones who give them this power and we will be the ones who are going to take this power away from them!"

Jack and Robert kept being shut and John and I did not understand how they felt the whole thing. All of a sudden, Robert said: "Abstinence is hard" The same thing that John's friend said the night before. Then Robert went on, this time more seriously: "Are you telling me that for one month we will stop hitting on girls and that we will only treat them as friends?" "Exactly!" I replied, visibly happy to see that Robert showed interest and perhaps even sympathy for the crazy experiment. "And specifically, how should we behave?" Asked Jack.

"Nothing strange or weird, for the duration of the Test we'll act with girls like normal friends chatting with them without trying to hit on them. We'll be friends and nothing more." "And what should I do if I see a hot chick in the club?" Robert claimed. "The experiment will be limited to girls who attend our school.

This is for two reasons: it's more than 1000 students in our school and the sample is representative enough. We should behave in the same way with girls from our school, inside or outside, this means in the clubs or any place else. Otherwise if a chick sees a different approach, she would think you're weird and might suspect something." Doubts were slowly dissolving, and after all, the point was to stop running after chicks for just one month. The curiosity was taking the place of skepticism. Robert and Jack, to my incredible surprise, proved to be involved from the beginning. I even found out that Jack had just been dumped by his girlfriend which he still felt something for and knowing that no one would have come to his ex, for at least one month, made him feel safe, somehow. Hunger stopped our meeting and we decided to see each other in the afternoon at the rehearse room where we used to play in our spare time. I took my Vespa and I got home, this time with less doubts than the night before. Jack and Robert have proved to be really confident and this reassured me. Perhaps the fear to be considered crazy was not so strong anymore.

Robert and Jack's presence extended the founder group of 6 and surprisingly in the afternoon at 4 pm in the recording studio, it was already 20 of us. Not bad, considering that in the beginning my proposal had been welcomed with skepticism and derision. I took the floor, as usual. I explained the project to the guys who didn't know anything about it yet. As we expected, since John, Robert, Jack and I, the most popular guys in the school and sort of icons for most, were the promoters, the other guys seemed to be quite convinced. Of course they came up with some doubts but John, with his great dialectic, answered every question. The group was slowly gathering around the project feeling near each other by the same problems of teenagers. The discussion ended up, we played some songs, drunk a few beers and went home pretending to study for the next day math test.

Saturday, September 17

The morning after I arrived at school and I started enjoying the benefits of popularity: the younger guys began to approach me and John to ask for information about the Test that was scheduled. The new was spreading around very fast and in less than two days a new group was born on Facebook and a few days after, every guy in the school know about it. In the following weeks, the Fantastic Four group (John, Jack, Robert and I, so we were called at school), answered the questions of curious guys. The excitement was increasing and with texting and the Facebook group everything got faster. In addition, spontaneous discussing groups began to gather. John assigned us four one of these groups: each of us was responsible for different grades. It really seemed that the project was growing at a pace we would have not expected. We were dedicating even less time to studying than before and the afternoons were devoted to detailed analyses of the Test while responding to doubts that came up. The Facebook group helped us communicating quickly and easily with every guy involved. The basic concept was simple but we still needed to give it a shape, rules, the necessary control system in order to grant an efficient general coordination. In other words, we had to be sure that no one was secretly hitting on girls. Just one false step from any of the guys and the consequent domino effect would have definitely spoilt the Test. Being the four most popular guys in the school assured us a good power over younger guys but we could not be sure that no one would have not broken the rules. To ensure that everyone respected the agreements, we promised that once the experiment was over, younger guys would have had our advice on how to pick up chicks. This is how we sold it to them. Everything was going pretty well until a text message of Giulia brought a lethal doubt: she and I were together. I immediately thought that the Test imposed me to treat her as a friend for a month but then I realized that she attended another school so that was not a problem. But, there was still a question to be answered: how should we act with relations which started before the Test? If they have continued dating, this could have undermined the success of the Test. On the other hand, if they didn't told anything about the Test to their girlfriends and treating them as "friend" for a month at the same time, well, this would have been no good. Jack had just been let down, so he didn't have to worry about it. Robert didn't have a stable relationships while John was had my same "problem": a girlfriend. Later that evening, we met to discuss the issue: the excitement was so high no one could stop everything right now. At the same time, ignoring girlfriends for a month was not the wisest thing to do. Obviously, the most important thing for the Test to be successful, was that none of the girls should have known anything about the project. No one. And obviously, again, John proposal to inform only our girlfriends about the Test was rejected. "Are you crazy? Telling even only one girl means every girl in the school will know about the Test in 5 minutes flat!"

We knew girls and the hope they could keep the secret was null. This was the only problem which could really undermine the success of the Test but after talking and talking we decided we did not care that much. We were interested to see what it would happen when the boys stopped to pay all the attention to girls who they didn't know yet: in case of existing relationships it was different. And we could not risk smashing all the couples in the school. So what we decided was: couples would continue their nice quite life and the single guys would not approach single girls. "Good, we found the right solution!" John claimed, in accordance to the general feeling of relief wavering on the Fantastic Four. We went home, feeling a little lighter knowing that we saved the Test.

Preparations were in progress and we kept wondering when the Test should have started. It was necessary that everything was ready and that every single guy was properly informed before the big start. Do it before or after Christmas holidays, this was the question.

CHAPTER 3

WHEN SHOULD WE START?

Monday, September the 19th

The following Monday, we met again in the yard for updates:

"Let's start before Christmas! By now everyone is informed and excited and if we wait too long to do so, the risk is that the general energy flops."

Robert claimed. In fact we had been informing the high school guys since a few weeks and trough chatting we reached almost everyone. The risk was that the excitement could have dropped so we decided to start the Test before Christmas. October was the right month to start. A whole month and at the end of it we could have come to conclusions. For 30 days the girls in our high school would have not received any attention from us. "A girl who does not receive attention, is a dead girl!" Jack joked. In fact, this was one of the things that the Test should have proven. What if all the guys stop spending so much time and energy to the girls? All the guys should agree with this: this was crucial. Once the starting date was set, we shared it with all high school students on Facebook, through text messages and word of mouth. It almost seemed that this project was a bit of help to all the guys in answering questions that everyone had. Probably the situation was the same for the entire male gender. I, with his initial proposal, had unveiled some doubts that it seemed to grip all males. The difficulties, however, were only at the beginning. We discovered that the staff organizing school parties (we let the younger students accomplish this task) has set a party for Saturday, October 15, the high school party. It seemed that they did not get the whole point. "Are they crazy? They think we're going to the party, drink and not hit on any girl?" Robert said and then continued: "It will be really hard for everyone not to hit on any girls for an entire month and if on top everything you set a party, how could they think we could keep our commitment?" I immediately replied: "It seems younger guys didn't get the point, I try to talk to them right now!" I met with one of the guys who organized the event. He explained to me that the party was already planned and could not be postponed due to previous agreements with the club.

"Why didn't you tell us about it before?" I asked him. "A girl will celebrate her birthday that night and asked me to keep the event secret until two weeks before to surprise her friends or so she said." "Knowing about the Test, you kept the secret on the school party just because a girl asked you?" I asked him, bothered. From his answer I immediately understood the situation:

"You know, it's a girl I have been trying to pick up for a while..." I asked immediately: "Did she lose her V-Card to you at least?" With his eyes down he said: "Not yet, she told me that if I had kept the event secret then..." "Then what? You already did her the favor." I replied. I was sorry to disappoint him this hard because I understood him but I did not want to ruin the test just because of his vain hopes. Ironically the Test was risking to blow up for the old same situation that pushed us to start it; maybe it was not that strange.

Anyway the problem seemed to be quite serious. It wasn't realistic to expect all the guys to stick to the rules with all the hot chicks from our school. And no exception could be considered. While I was thinking about the whole thing, I received a text from Giulia, she was asking to come over. I run there: I needed a break from all these doubts. I got there and I found here naked in the bed. That's why she called me. We made love with great intensity. Lying in the bed I started thinking how come that in certain moments girls and boys were so close and in some others a wall seemed to divide them. I thought that maybe I was thinking too much. Giulia saw I was worried about something and she asked me if everything was ok. "Are you ok?" "Yap! Don't worry." She could never imagine what we were plotting. Nothing would have really changed for me because I was in a relationship with her already. The big difference was for single guys. And it was ironic that it was John and I both in a relationship, who organized everything. Troubles were not over anyway. Beyond the party thorny issue,

John came up with a new doubt. He rang in that moment. "What if a girl approaches a guy?" He asked. After one minute of thoughtful silence, I tried to answer. "Well...actually, I don't know!" Great, clear ideas. "We want to see what happens if guys stop paying all these attentions to girls. But if a girl hits on a guy there's no reason for him to ignore her." "What if we insert this clause in the Test?" Replied John elegantly. "We should add that if a girl approaches you, you should ignore her exactly like they do with us very often. It is something normal for us guys but it isn't for a girl at all." "Well it could be interesting. We should find out what the other guys think; refusing a hot chick it's not that easy!"

"But it's not that common either!" Replied John. "Yes, well, I think you're right. Anyway, let's try. We already share the feeling for this Test. Let's talk to the other and start!" I left John and I immediately felt that adding this last clause was taking the whole thing into a new level. John and I informed Jack and Robert and all the other guys trough facebook and messages. And with our relief, our new proposal was pretty successful. October was almost there and we still had to manage the thorny question of the high school party. How could we manage that? Jack, Robert, John and kept thinking and thinking. Postponing it was not possible because arrangements with the club were already set. On the other hand, doing this party could represent a strong temptation for every guy and the experiment could blow up. The four of us got together in the rehearsal studio/room. "So what?" We said almost simultaneously. While we were there gripped by the doubt, one of the younger guy organizing the party ran inside telling us that the party could have skipped because of some problem with the alcol license of the club. Divine help? We weren't sure but it was obvious that no license, no party. Plus organizing it somewhere else in a such a short period of time was almost impossible. It seemed that fate was helping us. We left the rehearsal room happy and relieved and I went to Giulia's. We were seeing each other 3 times a week in that period, more or less regularly. Again, thinking about the nice relation we had, I asked myself why it couldn't always be that way between guys and girls. We understood each other in a snap and we were really having a good time together, after all. Probably the thing was that when you get into a relationship, gaps between sexes are less difficult or maybe each one tries to come to the other trying to understand the other one reasons. Oh well I don't know.

CHAPTER 4

THE RULES

Tuesday, September the 20th

I slept with Giulia that night and I woke up inebriated by the fragrance of her hair. The sun was high in the sky and I immediately felt that it wasn't that early. I looked at the alarm clock and I saw it was eleven! We completely forgot about time and everything but I thought that lying in the bed wasn't that bad. We laid together again and immediately after I took my iPhone and I saw two calls and two messages from John. I called him back immediately but he didn't answer: he was probably in class with our math teacher, that old hag. I took a shower, I told Giulia bye and once on my Vespa, I went to school waiting for John. I got there at 12:30 am right when all the students were getting out. John ran to me screaming: "What happened to you?" "I slept with Giulia last night and we just slept too late. Why? Any new?" "Yes, no party as expected. It's confirmed now."

"Great!" I answered. Day began pretty good, I thought. "Other news?" I asked.

"Nope. This is good enough." We decided to go for lunch together to discuss Test final details. Jack and Robert caught up with us. Old Simon came as well, we didn't see for a while. We had a giant pizza we couldn't even finish. During our binge we talked about all the details and we made sure everything was set.

After all, the Test was pretty simple and if everyone was respecting the rules, we wouldn't have any problems. We set all the main rules:

1 - trough the whole month of October, none of the guys would have dedicated any attention to girls with a second purpose. Relationship with the other sex would have been just friendship.

2 - If a girl would have hit on a guy, he should have refused any approach to go out with her.

3 - Regarding stable couples, nothing would have changed. They would have kept going on with their normal relations life.

4 - The Test would have involved just girls from our school.

This was all. Four simple rules for one month duration. This was the Test!

After lunch and after setting the four rules, we started spreading the message to everyone as usual. I thought that we were really dedicating a lot of our time to this project and it was clear that everybody was looking for concrete answers. Rules were transmitted to everyone trough text, Facebook and chat.

I couldn't stop thinking that maybe we were going far beyond mental sanity and we were pushing us to nonsense. I immediately understood that these were my normal doubts swirling in my head. "Fuck!" I thought... "Let's do it!"

Saturday, September the 24th

Saturday evening we met at the club ready to party hard. At every school year opening party, everyone was there, guys and girls. The night before I dreamt Giulia left me and I felt a little strange that night: I was afraid that dream could have been a premonition. Unfortunately, everything was real. During the party, with no clear reasons, Giulia told me that she couldn't go on with me and that she didn't feel anything for me anymore. I was speechless. I thought our relationship was pretty happy. I couldn't understand what was the reason that pushed her to change idea that fast. I set by myself for the rest of the night devastated by that unexpected break so pointless to me. Jack came by: "What are you doing here? Something happened?" I took a moment and then I answered: "Giulia left me and I don't even know why!" "What? Really? She left you this way, all of a sudden?" "Yes, she told me she didn't feel anything for me anymore." Jack has just lied down by his girlfriend and I imagined he could understand me very well. We talked about it all night long, paying no attention to the party in the club profused by music. At the end of the party, after Jack offered me his support, I got home sad and thoughtful but I was feeling a little bit better than before. Sharing my feelings with Jack made me helped me. The Test was getting a new meaning: I had always thought that it couldn't hit me directly because I was dating someone. I was free now and the all experiment would have concerned me very closely. Even if I could still feel the pain for the break up with Giulia, I started thinking that what happened could allow me to reach a new consciousness. I knew a could have more answers. After the party and assimilated the breakup, "time" came. We all together decided to officially start the test. Everyone was ready and informed and the energy fluttering around us was really incredible.

CHAPTER 5

THE CRAZY EXPERIMENT START

Monday, October the 3rd

After the eight o' clock school bell the Test started. Nothing would have really changed but our different approach with girls. This could have lead us to more answers and probably more results. What we knew for sure was that we couldn't have less results than now, I thought humming to myself. During the morning break of that Monday, we met in the courtyard to talk about the test and first feedbacks. Many guys reported that a friendly approach to girls who they were hitting on before made the girls react doubtfully. The were awaiting for the same old attitude from guys but from this monday the whole story was different. In very short time (just few hours) the situation was very different. A few girls felt weird from the distance guys were demonstrating towards them, guys that were hitting on them until the day before! I immediately thought how the situation could change in the long term. We just had to wait. And how the Test would have been for me now that I was a single again? Many doubts in my head but a strong curiosity for the future. For one month we would act in a different and coordinated way. The bell rang and we went back in, looking to girls in our class, trying to see if they understood they were part of an experiment. "We are crazy!" I thought smiling. After the first day, I arrived home quite thoughtful, as usual: I couldn't believe Giulia left me. I couldn't get the reason why: maybe the Test would have been helpful. While I was absorbed, as usual, by my thoughts I received a call from a private number. "Hello." I answered curious. "Hi, this is Martin one of the younger guys from your same school. Is Luke speaking, right?" "Yap, it's me." "I have a problem with the Test. There's a girl who asked for my number to some friends of mine because she likes me." "Wow!" I thought. We have just started with the Test and what we doubt it could happen, it is happening right now. According to the rules we set, he should have ignored her, not paying around with her. After all, all the guys accepted the rules even if theory was, of course, easier than reality. "Did she call you?" I asked. "Not yet. Plus she's very hot. I know the Test has started but ignoring her would be such a crazy thing!" I could completely understand him and couldn't blame him. but rules were clear. I could put myself in his shoes. The situation's timing was unpredictable. And what if this wasn't representing just a single case? "I can understand you perfectly. We knew this could happen and this is why we put a specific rule." We took on a big responsibility, I thought, but after all these guys accepted the rules of the Test so thy were aware of what they were about to face. "The only thing I can tell you is that respecting the rules is mandatory. I understand it's not easy but if we don't (respect the rules) we'll screw up the whole Test. Do not call her and wait for her to make the first move. If she does, if she calls you, well, you already know you can't sleep with her." "This is a fucking problem. You're telling me I should completely ignore her?" "I am afraid, yes, as girls often do. I know it's not easy considering that now she is hitting on you but the Test is more important, I'm sorry."

"I will be free to act the way I want after test, right? "Of course! Things could probably be even better than we thought. She sees you're paying less attention to her and she could be more attracted." "Listen, ok. I'll follow the rules and let's see." I didn't expect this strong support from this young guy. I thought desire would have been stronger. The Test had inspired us all more that what we've planned and made us more serious trying to get our answers. We were sharing the same condition. After I hang up, before I could put my iPhone on the table, another private call came in. I answered having the clear feeling that a similar problem could be the reason of that call.

"Hello." "Hi this is Mark from the school, Luke?" "Speaking, what can I do for you?" "A girl is hitting on me, what should I do?" I can't believe it, what is going on? Two similar and particular cases in the same day, the first day of the Test? What if the Test was causing this mental approach change?

Could this happen this fast? Old Albert (Einstein) said the time is relative. What I could see was that the whole thing was giving something to think about after just a few hours. What would have happen in a month? The following weeks I found out the both the guys who called me respected the rules. "Not bad, I'll take them out for a drink." I thought. After just a few hours from the start we already had some news. After school I met with John, Robert and Jack. I told them everything and together we discussed how easy this first part of the Test was demonstrating to be. Maybe not that easy for the guys who called me. Nevertheless, they told me they wanted to respect the rules, ignoring girl proposes. The Test in its authority was giving us rules that we had chosen ourselves and we had no other options. We had to stick to the rules. This kind of experiment was unique, never done before. A lot of crazy people hanging around but not as crazy as us setting up such a thing. News had only started, as I soon got to know.

CHAPTER 6

WHO CHASES NEVER WINS

I got home after the talk of the Fantastic Four and Giulia was waiting for me in the courtyard. "What the..." "Hi, I know what you're probably thinking but let me explain." "Explain what?? That you left me without a reason?!" "Wait, it's not that easy for me. I came here to explain a few things." I was a kind of confuse: first she left me apparently for no reason and then she came back even in front of my house all of a sudden. But most of all I was thinking either to ignore her or not as the Test taught: it could have been fun. Plus after our weird break up, I didn't feel like listening to her. She explained that she was living a difficult period at home: her parents were about to break up too and she was kind of worried about her future. I understood her even if being her boyfriend she could have told me everything from the beginning instead of leaving me and explain herself only after. We kept talking for a long time and I understood deep inside that we were still very close to each to other. It was clear that dialogue was everything, the key to our mutual understanding. During our talk I was struggled between Test rules, my feelings for her and a thousand other things. I really didn't know what to do. On one side I really crave to go back with her and this was really the perfect occasion. On the other hand, the experiment has just started and I didn't want to be the one messing up everything. This was exactly a situation not forecasted in the Test setting. We were sure we considered all the different possibilities but my case was beyond the rules we established. At this point, I should have decided how to behave. As usual, I went to bed thinking what was the right move. I could have probably talked to John next day and asking for his opinion. I fell asleep late with thousand of thoughts flowing in my head.

Tuesday, October the 4th

Next morning I got in school late so I couldn't get in my class before nine. And this time was pretty helpful. I hang around the school until I met a younger guy in the hallway who came to me: "Hi Luke, what are you hanging here during class?" "I was late so I am getting in at nine. What about you?"

"The same with me. Listen, I've got something important to tell you: there's a girl in my class who is tired...to be...well I think she decided to do IT very soon."

"Well, great kind of a new." I answered sneering. I knew what was coming next.

"...and she wanna do it with me!" After a few minutes of silence, I asked him: "Do you know the Test rules?" "Of course! Knowing them is not the problem, respecting them is the hard part." "Well, I understand. Something like this happened in these days. Actually yours is the third case lately. I am not sure whether the Test has something to do with all of this or the world is getting crazy. But you already now the answer. I can't tell you more. But just chill out: the good thing is that she won't do it with nobody else because all the guys must respect the rules so your appointment is just postponed to the end of October!" "But this is the point!" He said. "How can we be sure that nobody else is not going to hit on her. She seems kind of a determined." "Rules are clear and we all agreed on respecting them. I can try to look over the whole thing but I can't tell you anything more." "Is this it?" He asked surprised. "Yes, this is all." I answered. He seemed disappointed but honestly I couldn't help him more than that. Things were getting kind of a weird: three difficult cases to manage in a very short time already. The guy left and disappeared in his class; unfortunately I felt he wasn't persuaded and I was afraid he could have broken the rules. The probability of a girl who wants to sleep with you for the first time is near to the probability of a a sun eclipse. I decided to call up the Fantastic Four board to discuss the issue because one false step could vanish all the hard work and effort. We met in the rehearsal room that same afternoon. We weren't studying for school anymore because we dedicated all our spare time to the success of the Test. "It's hard!" Robert cried in order to break the silence and he continued: "In the beginning we couldn't get any decent result with girls although we were really focused on the "issue" and this is why we decided to try with the Test. Now that we stopped altogether, it seems like magically girls are chasing us. It makes no sense!" "We can consider this an interesting first lesson." I promptly replied, adding: "After just a few days, we've already learnt something." "Yes, what we've learnt is that we are fools because now we can't do anything anymore even if they beg us for it." Robert joked. We were both right. The first lesson we were taught wasn't priceless. We didn't have much to discuss for, rules were very simple and clear. The younger guy from the morning as like the others couldn't do anything before the end of October. The meeting was fast and brief. In the weeks after, the same younger guy, but not only him, went trough hell. He told us that the girl started paying "particular" attention to him and kept after him all the time. It was obvious that he was terribly suffering because he knew he couldn't anything and he began losing control. He told us that the girl whose name was Susan, was getting pushy in her approach. He described us an incredible scene that happened with her: he found her naked in boys locker rooms. Obviously it wasn't a mistake. It looked like the situation was about to boom and so we decided to step in. Actually we couldn't do that much but controlling from the outside that the general rules were respected and I understood it was very difficult myself. If I was in his shoes, I don't know how I would have reacted. Stated that the Test was the main thing, down to heart I wasn't sure that I could resist. Plus Susan was a hot chick. The good new was that Test was really giving interesting and surprising results. Most of all this fast and unexpected change of approach with girl was generating juicy consequences. Until then our old strategy, in all its variations, gave us completely disappointing results and now that we tested a total new approach (we stopped chasing girls, making us appearing more attractive) first results were showing up. After all, who chases never wins. I still had to come up with something to solve my situation with Giulia: how should have I behaved with her? Surprisingly, I came up with a very quick decision. I decided to fully respect the rules of the Test (even if I was living a very specific case) and to start ignoring her. Even if a part of me wanted to get back with her badly, I decided for the rational way leaving her the chance to come to me looking for reconciliation. If the Test was right, I would have been right. So I resolved myself not to chasing her anymore and to refuse her comeback in the beginning. I wasn't absolutely easy but I thought that risk was worth it. After all I loved to risk. A few days after things seemed to become stable and I had no news until that thursday, during the break in the school courtyard, a girl I hardly knew came to me.

CHAPTER 7

THE FIRST TEMPTATIONS

Thursday, October the 6th

"Hello, my name is Laura." She started. "Hi..." I answered a little surprised.

"I came here because I wanted to talk to you about a friend of mine who likes you and she sent me to ask your cell number." "I understand..." I honestly didn't understand if that was a joke or not. Considering last circumstances, everything was possible. I indeed decided to give her a chance aware of the fact that the Test rules were still valid. Laura went on: "Would you like to contact her if I leave you her cell number?" Rhetorical question, hoping that the girl was as cute as her friend Laura. On the way home thoughtful as usual, thinking about latest events: in such a short time things were getting interesting. In a few cases already, girls were proposing to guys although (or maybe that's was the reason why) we all stopped chasing them. I got home, had a quick lunch and I called the girl. The telephone rang a long time till a very sweet voice answered:

"Hello." "Hi, my name is Luke and I had your number from your friend Laura."

A few minutes silence passed, that she was ashamed or maybe she didn't expect my call this fast. "Hi, my name is Tiffany, I am glad you called me this soon." After another embarrassed seconds silence, I broke the silence:

"How come you sent your friend Laura ahead? I asked knowing the answer already. "You know. I don't know you that well and so I didn't feel like coming and talk to you on the spot." "Ok, I understand." I answered and said: "Do you wanna meet? "Sure!" She immediately answered like she was waiting for my proposal. "We can meet tomorrow for the morning break and talk a little bit."

"But I am not at school tomorrow, I have to see the doctor." She answered.

I had the feeling she wanted to see me in private. And most of all, I understood that I was breaking the Test rules. As a divine sign, while I was talking to Tiffany, I received a John's message. I waited till the end of the call.

"I am free this week end and Saturday can be perfect to see each other." I said sharply. "Yes, I would love to." She immediately answered. "I know a cute restaurant up in the hills. It's very nice and there's a beautiful city view." It could be something romantic, I thought. "Well, it seems cute, ok." "I'll pick you up in Vespa." "Ok then, I'll be there for 8 o'clock." "Good. I'll send you my address on Facebook, I sent you my friend request too." "Ok, so if we don't hit each other before, I'll meet you on Saturday." "Ok, see you on Saturday, bye!" She said with her sweet voice. "Bye!" I quickly answered. I interrupted the call and for some reasons I already knew what I would have read in John's message. I was again breaking the rules and I was pushing myself a little too far. John wrote that he wanted to meet with me that same afternoon to update on the Test developments. So I decided to get on my Vespa and I got to his house in a few minutes. He lived in a nice house with the pool and the atmosphere was pretty familiar to me because the summer before we had a lot of fun organizing many parties. We started talking and because of our good friendship I couldn't hide him my transgressions. "What did you do? Did you plan to go out with her?" Asked John, worried. "I know but how could I resist?" I asked hoping in John's understanding. "You should and that's all! It can't be you, who started and organized everything, to break the rules. If someone gets to know this, it's over." "I could think about not going but it would be hard." "We worked a lot to set and start the Test and to avoid for other guys to break the rules. Even the guy with the girl hitting oh him pushed back and everything was working perfectly. We can't ruin everything, now." "I know, don't think I am easy on this. I could cancel the appointment and save the Test success. Or go out with her and keep the thing secret. "There's no way you can keep it secret, she would talk about it with her friends immediately and you know girls. She probably already did it. "At this point, I can tell her that I can't go out with her and that we should re-arrange. But she will never understand why because I don't know what excuse tell her." "This is the best solution. Not the easiest, but the best. We still have a lot to learn and we are just at the first steps of the project."

"Ok, you are right. I tell her that I can not go out with her now. Let's give the Test the priority even if you can't understand how hard this is for me."

This was our deal: no appointment to avoid any damage to the Test.

I decided to call her immediately and take this off my mind. She was a little disappointed even because I wasn't able to give her a good excuse and I wasn't really persuaded." Actually, I could feel that she was a little sad and honestly I felt bad even because I really wanted to go out with her.

Trying not to think about it I met with the Fantastic Four that night. We went for a beer and we confronted each other on the Test results.

CHAPTER 8

A FIRST NEW AWARENESS

We all noticed that stopping running after girls, they started showing more interest toward the opposite sex sometimes even making the first move. We already proved ourselves that chasing didn't not give any results. We discussed about it all night long and we came to the conclusion that things, thanks to the Test, were getting better for all of us. Girls were starting to propose and now the problem was that we could not respond to these approaches. We cheered all together and we got in bed excited for what the Test could have saved for us. We have high expectation and we knew that we were on the right path for concrete answers.

Friday, September the 7th

The night was a good advisor. The next day I got up with a juicy idea which I proposed to John in the morning break in school. "We could stress the Test organizing a party where all the guys, in the same moment in the same place, should behave with the same rules of the Test." I said to my dear friend enthusiastically. "What?" You want to organize a part where guys have to stay away from all the girls?" "You got it!" "You really like to suffer and I don't know why!" He said smiling: "It's like trowing fresh blood in a piranha pool. Practicing in school (and we saw that it works) and organizing a party forcing the context are two different things, very different!" "I know but it could be interesting to see how the Test works stressing it all the way." I was a risky guy but John wasn't, he has always been a lot more rational. "I don't think this is a good idea, abstinence could prevail taking to dramatic consequences."

I realized that I was really starting to talk nonsense. Like if I was under LSD.

On one side, I was dying for pushing the Test to the extreme, making the experiment even more radical. After all before the Test started, even the idea looked crazy but at the end we all went for it. At this point, why not pushing it all the way to see what would have happened? John was evidently wiser and more well-controlled than me while I loved to risk just for the sake of it. All of a sudden, my dear friend came with an objection that caught me unprepared:

"You are telling me to push the Test when you are risking to break the rules with Tiffany?" I answered promptly: "Oh oh wait wait. I am not going out with Tiffany so I am not breaking any rules!" "Ok ok, I trust you, even if, I am telling you, she is hot!" Said John smiling. "Hey, what are you doing? Are you trying to hit me exactly when it hurts." I claimed keep joking. He kept talking immediately more seriously. "The fact is that everything now works and we should be happy about it, but we are playing with fire. If we radicalize the whole thing, I don't know what could happen. We could even blow up everything." Before I could answer, I got a text from Tiffany. She was saying she was sad that she couldn't go out with me on Saturday and she really wanted to meet me because I was cute. "Damn!" I thought. It was already hard to let her down and received her text made it even harder. Anyway, I answered to John: "You know I am a risky guy, you know me. The whole thing about the experiment is crazy but we're getting interesting feedbacks from it and I think that if we set the party for the end of the month, we could get a lot more things to reflect on. We talk about it again!" So we got quickly in class meditating on the Test final party. We were really near to the limit. On top of everything, I was living a thorny situation: Giulia on one side which I could get back with and Tiffany on the other side which was very cute plus she was a minor, which was picking me on. In both cases, I would have definitely broken the rules. I shouldn't have done this, I was one of the founder of the Test. During the last two hours of school, all these thoughts were wildly flattering in my head while I was sitting in my back seat. In front of me it was sitting Ilary, a "ooh

ooh" not bad classmate which that day was showing a hot tanga, peeping out her jeans. I was obviously hypnotized by that vision since I heard the bell ring. The Test together with Giulia and Tiffany dilemma, was making the situation unreal and extremely complex: how would I have behaved? Would I have been able to respect the rules all trough?

In the beginning of this adventure, I was with Giulia and maybe I thought unconsciously that the other guys could have been involved in worse problems, not me. But after Giulia left me, everything change and all of a sudden I was forced to respect the rules as everybody else. I realized that even if this was an obvious thing, it is true that the more you want something very often, the less you can get it. In this case, I was testing as well as the other guys that kicking dedicating attentions (or maybe worrying?) to girls, results all of a sudden were improving. I have to admit that we stopped spend negative energies, being scared and worried that were getting real as in a prediction (self-fulfilling prophecies). With this new approach, even without focused actions, results were immediately getting better and better. In other words, before the Test started, we were putting such a big effort but the attitude we were putting in place was a L-attitude because it was full of skepticism and doubts on the final result. We were approaching girls already knowing in the deep of heart that we were getting anywhere. We were not self-conscious enough and this was the reason why we were so this disappointed and frustrated. Now that the Test forced us to leave this dysfunctional behavior we were achieving a lot more than before, despite our total approach immobility. I immediately realized that this consideration was reasonable and that by sharing it I could have helped other guys. In the end this was the real goal of the Test. At the end of the lessons, it was raining outside. Damn. I was with my Vespa and my tires were a little slick. Before jumping in what it seemed to be the big flood, I talked to John about my idea I reflected upon while I was staring at Ilary's butt (incredible how a nice ass can help reaching such a high consciousness). I quickly gave him all the details and he immediately sympathized. The energy we spent in the past for girls proved itself to be negative energy because compromised by worries, fears and doubts (that we often were not conscious of) on the success of our efforts. And as a self-fulfilling prophecy, each time we weren't achieving anything. I immediately thought that the truth or answers that we often look for are actually very simple but not obvious and that therefore at the bottom line there are no secrets to achieve an objective but only new levels of awareness. John and I shared this new consciousness on facebook and from likes we noticed that almost everyone was agreeing. I felt great as this our new idea of the Test could help many guys in improving their relationship with girls. Everything started almost as a provocation but very quickly this was helping us giving new answers quite interesting.

CHAPTER 9

BREAKING THE RULES

While I was driving home with my Vespa, under a terrible storm, I remembered Tiffany has once shared her position on Facebook and I got her address.

Her house was not far from my way home. I got the turnaround and realized I was going straight there. I felt like an invisible force was driving my scooter (this was the second time I felt like I was under LSD). I got in front of her house, stopped and turned off my Vespa. Lunch time, not the best moment to ring in. "Ring the doorbell?" I thought. "What am I doing?" I thought ringing Tiffany on her iPhone was a better idea. She text me immediately like she was there waiting for my call. After a few messages she met me under the rain just out of her home. As soon as I saw her I realized I felt a strong attraction for her and I could feel my heart beating harder and harder. We talked a little and I lied again about Saturday. I was about to leave when, overwhelmed by attraction, we started kissing for a few minute which seemed ages. I immediately realized how sweet this was, how passionate, how nice. I left in silence. Rain has stopped and during the whole way back I could feel her taste of her kiss. Just after lunch I turned a little bit more rational so that I could understand I was the first person breaking the rules of Test! Nevertheless, I liked it so much that I thought it couldn't be that important and I decided not to tell John. I received a text from Tiffany who was telling me how much she loved that kiss we had. She said in a very sweet way that it was a long time she was waiting for it. I started worrying I couldn't stop the whole thing between us; that kisses and than those hot messages. All that was making me crazy. How could I resist to all those temptations? Well, actually, I knew what the answer was. Giulia got in touch me again, and this made the thing even worse. She wanted to see meet with me again, get a drink, have a little talk.

Lately, I forced myself to be less rational, and I immediately accepted her invite. The Test was making everything too hard, complicated. Now that I had more chances, they were useless. I realized what I shared with John was true: things were happening once I stopped worrying about them. I spent the all afternoon on Facebook chatting around till time for the drink with Giulia came. I felt a little strange: I didn't know what to think and didn't know what to expect from this confused and weird period. Giulia and I had a little chat till she said she wanted to go back with me. Gosh, things were getting really complicated! Anyway, as with Tiffany, I just left myself go. After the drink we went to her house and we made love whole night long. My transgression was getting shameless, I thought. I was in bed with Giulia and watching her naked beside me, all the doubts just flew away. I was sorry, on one side, because I was worrying for the Test success, but the more emotional side was incredibly satisfied and I was starting thinking that the real happiness came from this instinctive part. Tasting the fantastic taste of her lips, hugging and kissing in the bed, made me feel so good I forgot about worries. I couldn't ask for more in that moment. I stayed over for the night and the next morning I woke up in time to go home, pick up my books and flew to school in time to the 8 o' clock morning bell.

CHAPTER 10

PROGRAM CHANGE

Saturday, October the 8th

The morning went without twists and the end of the lesson came pretty fast. I was living my secret easily till I met Tiffany, out from school. She was there me near my Vespa, waiting for me, I supposed. "Shit!" I thought. Before the Test started I was so lucky to have a girl waiting for me after school.

"Hello!" She cried out with a quite satisfied smirk.

"Hi, how are you? I answered somewhat automatically.

"Yeah, everything ok, I wanted to see you." She said sweetly.

I didn't know what the f.. to do. We just kept talking without arouse any suspicion and I would be save. But I immediately realized that being next to her words were very few because attraction was too strong. In an pure instinctive push, I decided to take her by scooter in a park where we could kiss for hours away from indiscrete eyes. And that happened. I stayed there even after lunch time. We spent the whole afternoon together and she had to tell her mother a bunch of bullshits to stay out late that afternoon. Around dinner time I took her home and we said bye with a very intense kiss. It was clear that the situation was getting out of mu hands. I wasn't sure either to talk about this with John or not. The more difficult things were getting, the more difficult it was to talk about it with him but I knew I had to. I decided to talk to him anyway. His reaction, I was surprised, was incredibly rational, wise, calm. After all, I thought, he was my friend, and more than anything he was a male as well, therefore he could understand me very well. We talked about it on the phone for a long time with the promise of updating the following day in class. The good part was about to come. John himself confided me that he also had broke the rules a younger chick. He kept the thing secret. I immediately felt better. "How come we can't f... hot chicks or should we keep everything secret?" We very well knew the reason which brought us to the Test and we knew that we had to stick with the rules in order to justify the whole thing. Nevertheless we were aware of all we have done. It was so ironic that we were just the ones not to respect the rules, the two of us till now, as far as we knew.

Monday, October the 10th

The following Monday John and I had lunch together and spoke about this in a deep way. I felt better knowing that my friend was in my same boat even if the direction we had undertaken was the wrong one. We said good bye and on my way home I started thinking about Tiffany and Giulia. I really felt an incredible attraction for both, even if in a different way: I was sharing with Giulia a long and deep relationship that had made our tie solid while toward Tiffany, for now, I felt a just a pure physical attraction. I got home, tried to study just not to think about it but it was impossible. Last events were really turbulent. We were hardly half way to the end of the Test and the two promoters, John and I, had already broken the rules. Nevertheless, we were optimistic because up to now the experiment had allowed us to reach a higher level of consciousness.

We believed that this was shared also by most of the guys from our school.

What had happened till now had confirmed that our attitude in the past had always been ineffective because of our shifty lack of self confidence on a positive ending. We were acting with determination but we didn't really believed in ourselves. Only now we fully understood this. This was extremely useful in order to make us continue on the path of results we thought we deserved. John and I decided to keep our transgression secret even if this wasn't the solution. In order to put an end to the issue, we should have cut our "affairs". At least I could keep seeing Giulia, since I was dating her before the Test and besides, in spite of our breaking up, I had never didn't made the first move. Easy to say, but not to do it. John put an and end to his affair in a smart way while I was torn to pieces by the doubt. Even if I could go back with Giulia without braking the rules of the Test, I still had the Tiffany issue. The point wasn't that my relationship with Tiffany was so long and strong I could not break it up easily but the attraction for her was really irresistible and tremendous. Anyway, the point was I had already broken the rules and I couldn't go on this way. I was deeply thinking about the whole thing when my phone rang. I immediately answered and I had a long chat with a younger guy from my school who gave me new feedbacks on the Test evolutions. Useless to say, that while he was talking, deep inside I knew that I wasn't reliable. I had started the Test adventure with John and I was the first one not to respect the rules. But what the guy on the phone told me left me speechless. He told me that, according to his own experience, after the first phase in which the lack of attention towards girls had ironically helped him, now the girls themselves, realizing there was no more interest, started to ignore him openly. The point was that this development was shared by a lot of guys: the same thing was happening to most of us. I hung up and started to think: in the beginning of the Test and for the following weeks we have noticed how our change of attitude toward girls had caused a greater interest on their side. In the beginning, this seemed senseless to us but, after a deeper evaluation, we have noticed how the lack of attention towards girls made us appear stronger and had made us more easy in the relation. To cut it short, we had cut the vicious circle of uncertainness and doubts which took us away from the objective. Without meaning to, we had shown a more attractive and confident image of ourselves. This seemed us a great teaching and had pushed us to go on with the Test. Until this last call. I decided to call up the fantastic Four. We met in the practice room in the afternoon in order to discuss and try to understand if we had made any mistake. I was aware that I broke the rules and after talking to John I decided to share it with Jack and Robert too. They understood right away and decided that right now the most important thing was understanding the reason of this new feedback change on the part of the girls. "It is clear that not acting as chasers helped us in the short term but in the long one this kind of attitude won't grant us a lasting success." John said. I replied: "It can surely be part of a winning strategy but if you always show to be indifferent and unconcerned, in the long run the girl can deduce that you have no interest for her: the best that can happen will be to be ignored by her or what's worse she will perceive your disinterest which will cause resentment towards you". Jack added:" If a girl has interest for you and you show a certain indifference, as the Test teaches us, either you'll be thought to be gay or she will throw negative opinions on you". We all agreed about this and realized that the Test needed some changes in order to supply us with some useful cues of reflection. If we had continued like that, a certain conflict would have started in the relations between girls and guys without anything useful to think over. It was time to refresh our experiment: we were the founders and we decided to give a different imprint to it. First of all we needed to go deeper in the relation with a girl to be able to understand many other aspects neglected up to now: in other terms, if a guy simply ignored a girl without trying to develop a slight personal relation, it was impossible to understand other dynamics involved. It was time for the 2.0 Test version. The rules were perfect and showed to be efficient up to now in giving us the first important teaching to reflect on. Moreover the participation to the Test and the respect for the rules had been perfect, except for me and John. Now it was the time to introduce a new changes in order to obtain useful feedbacks from the Test itself. After the first phase where our new common attitude led to important results (even if it wasn't possible to take advantage) now it was necessary to change something in order to keep the Test alive. We came to the conclusion that the evolution to which we assisted was normal: in the first period, stopping chasing girls, we transmitted, without being really aware, an image of ourselves more secure and attractive. It was clear that this could not last forever. Showing ourselves more rational and distant could improve short term results but this approach needed a step forward and a new strategy that could lead us to concrete results. The main objective, now that our new "distance" strategy was working, was to try to find other strategies that could make us obtain better results with girls. In other words while in phase one of the Test we all wanted to gather information in order to make considerations, now after the first results, we wanted to use what happen to help us create strategies which could improve our relationship with girls. The experiment started blindly and we did not know what to expect: now that our ideas were clearer we wanted a change. The question was: "How can we use what we had experimented until now in order to let us discover concrete strategies that can help us improve the approach with the opposite sex?" We can say that in the beginning everything somehow started as a joke (even if it wasn't really like that) and now the little change in direction allowed us to give everything a more serious twist so that at the end of the month all the guys from our school could have concrete tools to improve their relationship with girls. "Wow!" I thought. I never imagine that my first idea could become extremely serious and helpful to everyone. Somehow this new approach came from a deeper consciousness and I liked it because feeling helpful to others was pushing do better and to deeper analyze the issue. Plus if we found useful strategies this could be a good way to pay back all the guys for their collaboration to the Test and their respect to the rules. We kept confronting each other on the matter until we came to an interesting conclusion: before the Test started we were not sure because we thought that this was weird enough to make us appear crazy (in the best case). Actually we were experimenting that every time you follow your instinct, in spite of the fact that it seems rational to do so in the beginning, you find yourself in situations never lived before that push you to grow and improve yourself. My initial idea to create this Test was crazy in the beginning but growing in this small project and facing normal fears brought us to newer and high consciousness. Before the Test we were going out every weekend with aim to pick up some nice chicks without the necessary self confidence: we were always adopting the same tactic without correcting eventual mistakes. My idea, from pure instinct, was allowing us to get answers and useful ideas on which to base new issue. As the first night we could feel we were sharing the same feeling towards the initial Test idea that we never shared before in a conscious way, now the feeling was very similar if not the same. The all four of us were on the same frequency: it was time to use this new level of consciousness in order to grow and, at he same time, helping all the guys from our school in a very deeply felt issue as the way to approach girls. In the end, helping ourselves, we would have allowed many others to have real answers and this was really gratifying us. We all agreed in considering the first part of the Test profitable and over. We also agreed in changing pace in order to have more answers: it seemed like we only had time before the Test ending to get to useful conclusion for us and other guys. In a few words time was rushing. We could feel the energy in the air as the synergy and the tension between us four: this was gratifying and making me feel stronger. But the Test itself was still giving us a strong thrill softened only by everyday life. After this first step we decided to get deeper.

I started "We all agreed till now on what above said: it's time to get deeper, now. Do we want to change the rules? Or keep them the same, adding a few details?" Robert immediately answered: "I think that if we maintain them the same nothing will change and we will not be able to modify the Test. Everything will go on in the same way up to now." Old Robert was actually right. Rules prevented us from renewing the Test as needed. I thought that more flexibility was necessary, in other words we had to leave the guys free to text girls making them see the interest without going deeper. As soon as I presented my idea, wise John highlighted me something important: "The Test worked because we prevented every real involvement. If we loosen the rules things could get even harder for the guys because they would get nearer to the purpose without having the chance to go further. I immediately answered: "Otherwise, if do not change the rules leaving the guys to be more involved, we could never have better answers. I think the change is unavoidable. Freeing the guys a little more, with some limits, we can experiment strategies."

Jack continued my consideration: "Actually we should play around a little bit with girls flirting as they often do with us, in order to see what works and what doesn't." Everyone nodded after Jack speech: we literary had to provoke girls letting them think we were interested without going deeper. On one hand it would have been fun but on the other hand we were playing with fire: getting closer to the goal without reaching it, would have been a real torture! John and I almost in one voice admitted how we had broken the rules when these were too strict. If now we reduced restrictions, more guys would risk to go beyond the limit. At the same time we understood that taking some risks was necessary and we decided to walk on the path of liberty: it was anyway necessary to set new rules or add some variations to the existing ones. "I think that adding variations to the existing ones, will be the best choice. Rules are clear enough already and if we just add a little variation it would be easier for everyone to respect them." I immediately claimed. After the general agreement we took out the paper of the rules:

1 - For the whole month of October none of the guys would have given attention to the girls for other purposes. The relationship with the opposite sex would have been based on pure friendship.

2 - If a girl tried to hit on a guy, he would have to refuse any appointment.

3 - In case of stable couples nothing would have changed. They would have continued their love story.

4 - Just girls from our school would have been involved.

Dirty old Robert said: "We could let the guys, even myself (he said smiling) get up to a kiss without chances to go further. For example, if a girl has some interest for a guy and makes the first move, the guy can text her on the phone, chat with her on Facebook and see her without going further than a kiss."

He kept on, sure of his proposal: "If the girl shows to want to sleep with him, he will have to stop her and keep her playing along. Probably in doing all this we can have many feedbacks to set winning strategies. In any case the girl cannot sleep with anyone else so that the combination between the guy's refusal (and the demonstration of self consciousness as seen in the first part of the Test) and the lack of competition will probably push the girl to ask herself how to behave and maybe keep persisting with the guy till the end of the Test."

"What a smart analysis!" Said Jack joking, arising hilarity. By the way Robert's idea wasn't that bad. The guys would have been free to play with girls (once again as they are used to do), exchanging telephone numbers, texting on the phone, chatting on Facebook with the usual limit of the kiss, not beyond that.

We thought that by doing this we could develop a minimum relation between girls and guys getting more information to work on. After all, this was all that happened between Tiffany and me, and I felt a little better thinking that while I was breaking the rules I I was just anticipating the new changes (at least this is what I wanted to believe). I felt even better thinking that thanks to the new changes I could keep seeing Tiffany in the same way I did up to now without going further. While I was deep thoughtful, Jack said something interesting:

"By doing this, we will allow the guys to loosen up a little bit and at least petting with some girls after this long abstinence!" There was a general laugh and John said: "We have to remember that the guy shouldn't do the first move, as it has been up to now, and you can only get to the kiss if the girl approaches the guy."

"Right, of course, no doubt" I said too.

We drew up the rules of the 2.0 version of the Test.

1 - During the last weeks of the month October no one would have shown any attention to the girls for further purposes. The relation with the girls would have been based only on friendship.
2 - If a girl tried to hit on a guy, he could give her his phone number, text and chat with her on Facebook and get up to a kiss, nothing more.
3 - In case of stable couples nothing would have changed, they would have continued their love story.
4 - The girls involved would have been only the ones from our high school.

The only variation concerned the second rule: a wider freedom was allowed with the risk that the rules could be broken (even if the risks were neutralized by giving some air to the guys) granting at the same time more information in order to set strategies that could help us more. Changing this only rule, we wouldn't make thing more difficult, allowing everyone to understand it deeply. Once the meeting was over, we decided, like before, to share the new on Facebook so that all the guys from the school were informed in a short time. We parted and as soon as I got on my Vespa I received a message from Tiffany. I felt a lot better thinking that I wasn't breaking any rule, in fact my behavior had been legalized. The message said that she wanted to see me. The same with me, after all, even more now that I was respecting the rules. I could test myself with Tiffany without going further than a kiss to find strategies that would have helped myself in the first place in the relation with girls. Anyway, I was aware that, since she was so cute, it would have been hard to stop at a kiss but now at least I would't have broken the rules. After all It was just a question of a two-week Test, and then I could have literally gone deeper with her. I replied to the message telling her I would have picked her up downtown since she was there with some girlfriends.

CHAPTER 11

NEW RULES

I turned on my Vespa and I split out. In ten minutes I was in the parking where we had to meet; while I was waiting I felt a hand on my shoulder. I turned, ready to meet the Tiffany's sweet look but what I saw was...Giulia! "Damn!" I thought. I was afraid that if Tiffany saw me with Giulia, she wouldn't want to go out with me anymore. "Hi!" Giulia said with an unusual sweet voice. "Hi." I answered, totally unprepared. She was there with Chiara, her blond friend who always had a crash on me behind Giulia's back. Chiara and I had fun the summer before but we decided not to tell Giulia. My pleasant thought towards Chiara was immediately interrupted. "What are you doing here?" Giulia asked me. Every time she was looking at me with those blue eyes, I felt uncomfortable lying to her. I didn't like to tell her lies, but I thought it was necessary sometimes. Before I started dating Giulia, I was completely honest with all the girls I was going out with and frankly it didn't help that much, not as much as I thought. "I'm waiting for John!" I automatically answered and not fully convinced."And what are you doing?" She insisted, pushing me to to resist even more to her deep inquiring look. "Nothing, well we were just walking around down town, nothing special, really." I tried to cut it short: on top of everything Chiara was wearing some killing leggings showing her beautiful butt and this was making everything even harder. "Ah...and John lost himself?" She continued, not obviously satisfied by the answers I gave till that moment. "He's coming, he just had to stop in a store and I didn't want to go with him." I gave a general and quick answer hoping she would have stopped her interrogatory. Despite the situation I was happy to see her because what I felt for her was still very deep and I was thrilled by the scent of her hair that was inebriating me as in our best days. We had our problems lately but still the passion between us was alive and I didn't want to stop our relationship. She was going trough a hard period, her parents were almost separating (they didn't at the end) and I could understand she was confused. My ideas weren't that clear either. Giulia was a nice and sensitive girl and she was different from anyone else: what I felt for her was something I never felt for anyone else and even Tiffany was nothing more than an affair. Time was running and higher the risk that Tiffany could appear; plus John would never come demonstrating that I lied to Giulia. My effort to cut the conversation fail when Chiara started talking about the Saturday night party in a club nearby and of how one of her friend was complaining about the lack of attention from the guy she wanted to go with. I smiled and luckily they didn't get it. I thought how ironic it was that Giulia and Chiara were involved in the Test without knowing. Chiara's friend was a victim of the Test and she was suffering by the effects of it. While I was thinking about this, while Chiara and Giulia were talking, I saw Tiffany come from behind their backs. "Holy shit!" Even though I felt like living in a limbo with Giulia (because she left me) I felt and I knew that we were going to get back together in a short time. Anyway I didn't think it was a good thing for her to meet Tiffany. Tiffany too, meeting Giulia, could decide not to see me anymore. "What a mess!" I thought. I didn't have time to think about a quick way out because Tiffany was almost there behind Giulia and Chiara. Game over!

"Hi Luke!" Little Tiffany shouted. Giulia and Chiara immediately turned to see where that sweet and delicate voice was coming from. I didn't answer immediately aware that as soon as I greeted her I would have confirmed our friendship. I was in a jam. As soon as Giulia and Chiara noticed Tiffany and stared at her from head to toes (this took just a few seconds) they turned back to me to see my reaction to the stranger arrival. "Hi." I was forced to say. I didn't see how Giulia felt seeing Tiffany and viceversa. I introduced Tiffany to Giulia and Chiara hiding my embarrassment or I thought so. After a moment of general silence and hardly hiding tension, I tried to say something in order to lighten the atmosphere, "Tiffany is from my same school." I just said. In some way I realized Giulia understood that Tiffany and I weren't just school friends.

Actually Giulia and I weren't going out together but I could bet she would be happy to know what was going on between Tiffany and me. Confirming my intuitions, Giulia excuse herself and left with Chiara. I felt a nice relief and I immediately looked at Tiffany to see what was her reaction. She didn't say anything at first but then she asked me the lethal question: "Was she your girlfriend?" I decided to be fair, thinking it was the best and easiest thing to do. "Who Giulia? Yeah, we were together but not anymore." "Oh ok, so you left each other?" "Yes, were are not dating anymore." I quickly answered. She didn't look particularly surprised nor worried. Maybe I was too worried myself. I had my answer at the end of the day, after we spent the rest of the afternoon together in the park. Sticked to the rules of the Test I just kissed her without going further. When I got home I had dinner and decided to call Giulia to hear how she was feeling about it. We were not together but we were about to and that afternoon I felt dead she did't like to see me with another girl. It was a long call almost never ending and we used it to remember all the nice moment that we shared. After talking so long, I felt that meeting Tiffany didn't hurt her that much and I felt better. Push by passion after the call I got on my Vespa and I went to her house for a happy ending. We spent the night together as we used to do and the next morning I took her to school.

Tuesday, October the 11st

She got off in front of her school, we kissed passionately and she asked me if I would have picked her up at the end of the lessons. I immediately said yes.

I got to school and while I was closing my Vespa John came to me and going into class he told me that the guys from the school welcomed the variations to the new rules. We could finally go a little bit further with girls and this on one side allowed us to have some few more answers and on the other one to satisfy some instinct we had to hold in the last weeks. The first part of the morning was pretty calm, nothing happened and I spent the whole time on Facebook checking guys reactions and considerations on the Test. Meanwhile I kept looking at Ilary who was sitting in front of me wearing that killing tanga under her jeans, again. During the break Ilary turned to me: I thought she saw me staring at her but she started talking about Saturday's party, the same party Chiara was talking about the day before. The party would have been in a club nearby, 10 euro for a drink and it seemed it was worth it. She asked me, in an alluring look in her eyes, if I would have gone and I answered I didn't know.

I felt her question was not an accidental question from a simple friend. I immediately imagined our kiss on the dance floor with the loud music stunning us. With this pretty pleasant image in my mind, I met John in the courtyard during the break. Jack, Robert and Old Simon joined us too. We shared our impression on the Test developments and on the fact that now that phase number 1 was over, we should have focalized on new rules and the related strategies we could elaborate which, by the end of the month, could help us and all the guys from the school relate with girls. I exposed what I read on the Facebook Test group and I confirmed new acceptable rules to the other guys. We agreed on the fact that we could get to a french kiss, it would probably help us to better understand many things finding new efficient strategies. Most of all, we had to carefully observe how girls would react from the complete lack of attention to new ones all of a sudden. I thought that, anyway, the transition from the first part of the Test and the second one would have been pretty instinctive and this made me feel easy. After all, the first part of the Test lasted just two weeks and now the transition to a new phase was happening in the right, period, I thought. As we proved to ourselves through the first part of the Test, we now had useful consideration inputs: girls started approaching us and showing themselves more interested thanks to this new strategy which made us feel more self confident and less needy. Whole this allowed us to to reach the awareness that: "Who ceases never wins." Before the Test, indeed, no matter if we were conscious or not, we were perpetuating the same behaviors over and over again: we were approaching girls without being conscious of our strategies, but acting random giving a sense of instability and no determination which led to a lack of allure for the opposite sex. The Test thought us many things, the most important of them was the mental attitude that we used in the past: lack of self confidence and an implicit demonstration of need which girls didn't show to appreciate. Most of all, we were missing an honest result analysis and a consequent strategy change: we were going random, and then complaining if we didn't see any results. That's typical of human being, I thought. We spoke of that during the whole break and we all agreed on these considerations. I perceived a feeling of great satisfaction and happiness in the air, since only two weeks had passed from the start of the Test, actually, we were only half way, everybody felt to be more "mature" and more aware which would have helped us in our relation with the girls. Thinking about my situation, in spite the slight confusion of the last period, I felt like smiling with pride considering the results obtained: I was about to get back with Giulia, I was keeping in contact with Tiffany and Ilary herself had shown some interest. Whole this was obtained with less than half the effort that I was dedicating before the Test, when the results were ridiculously inferior. The bell rang and I entered my class with a wide smile on my face.

CHAPTER 12

INCREDIBLE RESULTS

Chemistry teacher didn't show up so at the end of the break I decided to go out in the corridor and walk around trying to get new ideas on the Test development and mine too: while I was thinking I met Ilary who was magically walking around too. She talked about the Saturday party again, telling me that she could put me in the list. I felt like her pry was a declaration of strong attraction towards me. All the consideration that came out from the Test gave me a stronger self-confidence and now a girl showing interest in me wasn't an exception anymore.

We had a little talk about the party till she came nearer and nearer while the conversation was going on. No doubt I felt a strong attraction to her: my heart beat started accelerating. Physical proximity gradually grew till she put a hand on my hip with an excuse. It was so clear what the next step would have been.

Overwhelmed by the attraction and Ilary's sensuality and aware of respecting the rules, I finally let myself go. We kissed passionately for a few minutes. I honestly never thought I could kiss Ilary among all my class mates. These moments with her were simply divine. I enjoyed her wonderful taste and the magic smell of her hair through my hands without considering her perfect shaped body. Again, I understood that letting yourself go and leaving the deepest pulse live inside you, you could reach higher pleasure and fulfillment levels. Body language, I always thought, was a lot more effective to express many feelings and to put people in relation. In this case with Ilary I had a pleasant confirm. We often talked in the class and joked but never going beyond simple friendship as classmates.

I've always thought she was cute and sexy but I never thought we could end kissing in the school. If we had let our instincts express from the beginning, we could have live many leisure occasions, I thought. "Too often the fear stops us from risking and from daring beyond our comfort zone." In this case with Ilary, pure attraction had the best and overcame our mutual fears. If I hadn't asked for a date in the past, that was due only to my fears irregardless of the way I wanted to justify it to myself.

That free hour from class we spent together showed to be one of the most enjoyable moments in the last months. I also had the chance to touch her marble butt and I found it irresistible. At the end we put ourselves together and went back into the class as nothing had ever happened. We spent the last hour sharing complicity looks and when she was turning her back I couldn't but admire her beautiful tanga showing between her buttocks. I really enjoyed this pleasant break even if I could not go further. I was sure that with a girl like her I surely could have had sex in short time. But the rules were clear, and I didn't want to break them again. At the end of the day I went down to the courtyard and Ilary followed me to the scooter. I obviously liked it and actually I was enjoying this period of fervent results coming from a new mentality, as I understood. We decided not to kiss right there near my Vespa to avoid to be seen by someone from our class who would gossip around the following days. So I decided to have her sitting in the back of my scooter where a while ago there was Tiffany and took her to the same park where I went with Tiffany. "By the way, what was up with Tiffany?" I was wondering while I was driving all speed to the park with Ilary hugging my hips sitting uncomfortably behind me while slaloming among the cars in the traffic. I hardly had the time to think about Tiffany when I received a Sms that I read at the traffic lights. She said she wanted to see me even if I hadn't contacted her from the last time.

I immediately thought that she was looking for me in spite of my lack of attention for her (in the last days) but immediately I understood that things were working with her thanks to this lack. The "old Luke" would have been a lot more available for her, looking less attractive and I was conscious that part of this being always present because I wasn't so sure that she wanted to go out with me. I thought: "If I am always available I will get to go out with her." And this was something absurd that was hiding my fear. I was afraid that if I didn't constantly keep on touch I would have lost the chance to go out with the girl of the moment. Showing to be less available, not being the first to text or call her made me more attractive and Tiffany herself showed more desire to see me.

This consciousness which was neither innovative nor revolutionary was what we guys already shared after the first part of the Test. The second part would have confirmed this theory giving us at the same time useful strategies: the most important thing was the change of mentality. I've always been convinced that what makes the difference in life is the mentality and the approach towards situations and people we meet on our way. Very simple but too often undervalued or not properly considered. Concerning relationships with girls we already noticed how simply modifying our mental attitude, we were getting results more easily. Obviously this change at mental level didn't come in a conscious way but simply as a consequence of the Test and its rules. If we never started with this bizarre experiment, we would have never find a new way, more satisfying. I thought I would have ever been grateful to my initial idea. The light got green, so I went towards to the pleasant park with Ilary who was tighter and tighter to me with her head nicely lying on my back.

We got to the park, locked my Vespa and we started walking inside the park. In that moment I particularly high: the awareness achieved thanks to the Test (in a continuos improvement process), the consequent results and that special moment thanks to Ilary, made me the happiest guy in the world. We laid down in a quite place and we "had some fun together"; she was really hot. Her taste her perfume her body, sculptured by Michelangelo. I had a great time like I never did in the past. All of sudden, Ilary stopped, she looked me in the eyes for a moment and said: "You know Luke, you're very cute and I don't know why, in the past, we had never enjoyed ourselves like we should have." Then she added joking. "You could have caught my signals before. It was rather obvious that I was interested in you and still I am." "Signals?" I asked half in jest.

"Come on, all those looks, all those times when I got in your arms while we were joking in school. Did you really think I was acting only as a friend?". While she was talking I was still enjoying her taste in my mouth. "Well, I thought we were just joking. Let's say that I have always liked you and....." She interrupted me: "Do you think I didn't realize that you were watching me from behind, that you were watching my nice butt during lessons?" She said smiling. I shared the smile trying to hide my embarrassment. She kept on: "Why haven't' you ever invited me out?" "I don't know, I didn't think you could have been interested, Ilary". Ilary again "But you said you liked me." In that moment, after those words, thanks to the new mentality, I realized how in the past I actually had never asked her out for the simple reason that I was afraid she didn't accept or that she had no interest for me. In the past I would have told my self that in the end she didn't any interest in me. Just to justify my complete lack of action but the truth was that I was hiding my insecurity. After this consideration, in no time, I answered: "You are right but what matters by now? We are here together now." Then we started kissing with great rapture lying on the ground, in the middle of a field. I enjoyed the moment and the message she had transmitted, that she had been interested in me for a while, couldn't but fill me with pleasure. We enjoyed the situations typical of adolescence, I took her back home and we kissed again near her house and said goodbye. While I was flying on my Vespa along the beltway towards home I realized to feel really great. Adolescence was a weird period but, if you live it well and at the top, it could really give intense and unforgettable emotions. I wore my earphones and listened to a song that I had composed myself: "Get Down" that I had already put online on my site: www.LucaGrisendiArt.com I felt complete, light and free like never before. Could this feelings really come from the Test? The only thing I know is that for the first time in my life I had no worries and I felt like flying.

CHAPTER 13

CHIARA FACTOR

I got home, put my Vespa in the garage and while I was entering the sitting room I received a SMS from Giulia. She wanted to see me that same night: a shiver of pleasure crossed my back and without hesitation I said yes. I had dinner and got ready to reach her. I couldn't avoid thinking of how more she was looking for me in respect to the past weeks thanks to my new attitude: I was less available, she even saw me with Tiffany some days before and this made me terribly attractive and desirable to her eyes. While I was thinking about this with a smile of satisfaction on my face, John called me.

"Luke, Luke I've got important news! Tomorrow morning come to school a little earlier so I can update you!" "Incredible!" I thought. Besides the fact that John rarely expressed so wildly his enthusiasm, the telephone call reminded me the first night that we met to talk about the Test and everything started.

"Ok, ok, I'll be at school earlier!" I said, keeping the energy high. He told me that he had to go therefore the telephone call stopped there. Usually I arrived at school late or at the sound of the bell but considering the news, I decided to arrive early, for once. I went to Giulia even more charged up because of the imminent news that seemed to be rather interesting. It goes without saying that the night was just at its start. Once I got to her place, she was waiting in the courtyard even if the temperature wasn't that high. "Wow!" I thought. "When was the last time that she showed me such an interest?" We started kissing right away and we almost couldn't go up the stairs embraced to each other. We hadn't had this overwhelming passion for a while. We got to her bedroom on the upper floor and made it twice. She was alone at home therefore we could let ourselves go without problems. After the sex, we started speaking about our situation. She was very sweet and sensitive in that moment and her big blue eyes made me feel so tender and to such a degree that I couldn't but listen to her very carefully. As I had already understood, she had left me just because she was living a hard period with her parents who were separating. They didn't in the end so she calmed down and now she felt she was ready to get back together. Considering the last happenings I wasn't sure that getting back together was the right thing to do: now without too much effort I had around me more girls than in the past, therefore with some work and a new attitude I could have really had a great time. I didn't feel to get back with her and then feel guilty if I decided to go out with some nice chicks. Anyway one side of me, as always, desired to get back with her. It's incredible to see that as soon as I stopped thinking (or I'd better say worrying) about our getting back together, she herself would immediately approach the issue. It was clear by now that it wasn't the action in itself that made the difference but the right approach: in this period that I was acting rather cool and indifferent, I was getting much more than in the past. To be fair I decided to postpone my decision, being aware the wait would have increased my value to her eyes. By now I had absorbed the new mentality. I slept at her place and in the morning I decided to hurry up to get to school on time and enjoy the news from John.

Wednesday, October 12nd

I unusually arrived at school early, a new sensation never felt before. This time I didn't have to dash into my classroom. I joined John in the hall where he had gathered some school mates to share opinions. As soon as old John saw me, he invited me to join them and started to explain the first news of Test 2.0: thanks to the conclusions got from the first part of the Test, all the guys of the school now had a new attitude in approaching girls, surely more functional. Now that the rules were not so strict, it was possible to get deeper and some results were showing already. The guys confirmed that they had got more success with chicks during these last weeks than the previous months: John and I were really happy to have contributed to this result. The bell rang which meant the beginning of the lessons. I was still waiting to know what was the news that made John so excited the day before: he told me to wait for the break when we would have met in the courtyard with Simon and Robert to speak about the issue. I couldn't wait to know, I was too curious but I had to wait until the end of the third hour. I tried to be delighted by admiring Ilary's sculptural butt in front of me and thinking about the afternoon spent together and the petting at school and a mocking laughter was imprinted on my face. It was so evident that the chemistry teacher asked me about it: "Does the plate tectonics make you so happy? You would be the first one." She said with a hint of humor. I didn't answer and she kept on teaching: I was so deeply absorbed in my thoughts that if she hadn't asked that question I wouldn't even know what she was talking about. Ilary and I played with our looks for the whole lesson: she even passed me some "winking" notes that excited me a lot. Unfortunately, according to the rules, I couldn't go beyond kissing and this started getting too tight. I couldn't but admit that the rules of the Test, even if less strict, represented an obstacle already after the beginning of phase 2. In the first part of the Test it took longer to feel the limitations of the rules: I considered this sign as a continuous and more and more rapid improvement on my part which lately was generating pretty interesting results. The first lesson was over and we were waiting for the teacher of the second lesson when Ilary went out of the class. I couldn't but follow her, literally caught by the attraction for her. Without saying a word we withdrew into the place where we already a great time and we repeated the unforgettable experience. She had a breathtaking body and an irresistible perfume. We stayed there a long time. Then we went back into the classroom but we decided not to enter together, to avoid the eventual chattering that could have caused. Unluckily the second hour of lesson already started. Ilary went back in first, I don't know what she said. After few minutes I went back inside too and I told the teacher, who asked where I had been, that Robert and Jack had called me for an important thing regarding the school.

She believed my words and didn't ask for more. I realized my schoolmates started understanding what was going on between me and Ilary but I decided, very simply, not too care too much. Going back to my seat I saw Ilary's cute face smiling at me and I felt the irresistible push to jump on her but I obviously hold my self back. During the break, I went down to the courtyard with John so anxious to enjoy the news but I was disappointed: he withdrew with a chick he was intreated in in this period, notwithstanding my strong desire of knowing what was going on. I went towards the center of the courtyard and saw Tiffany with her school mates. I started dreaming about them while I decided to look for Robert and Jack. I didn't go to speak to Tiffany on purpose, I wanted to see if she would come towards me. I hardly had the time to think when I heard a sweet and delicate voice behind me: I turned back and realized how short was Tiffany. I loved the short chicks wearing Converse shoes.

"Hi Luke, what are you into?" She asked innocently.

"Hi! I'm hanging around here." I answered quickly.

"Are you looking for Giulia?" She asked maliciously with a hint of jealousy.

"Oh no, I'm not looking for Giulia: I'm looking for a girl of the second grade, short, with Converse shoes who, some day ago, was wearing a T-shirt with the writing "tonight I'll be good" even if it was afternoon. Can you help me?"

"Well, I think so. Come with me!" She said pretending not to understand.

We headed towards the scooter parking area, far from indiscreet eyes. I had understood what was going on. Actually things were going really well for me therefore I wasn't too surprised for my good results. We withdrew on a bench where nobody could see us. Profusion of kisses, petting and free play of hormones. I realized how sure she was of herself (she had the initiative of literally taking me out of the crowd) and how passionate once she removed the 'good girl' mask. When the bell rang we entered our classrooms. This was the fourth hour of school and I already had petting with two cheeks, more than I had in the whole last school year! "Was it possible that the Test had waken up all this potential in me?" I thought. If it was like that, "What in the hell did I do during all these high school years?" I deeply thought about it with Tiffany's taste still in my mouth. Back in class for the rest of the morning I could see Ilary looking at me as a wild cat. And I couldn't keep myself by looking at her cute butt hand crafted in marble. She knew it and she was flexing on purpose to show her tanga coming out from her tight jeans. The whole thing seemed so exciting to me that I could never pay attention to the lesson. As a matter of fact I didn't listen to the professors in the next 2 hours. Ilary started sending paper messages asking for my plans for the afternoon. "She's old style." I thought. We could easily chat on Facebook or whatsApp not being noticed. She was trying to make me understand that she wanted to see me....at her house. We would be alone till the evening and even a jerk could understand what she meant. As in the first part of the Test I was pushing myself beyond the rules, so now, despite more freedom Test 2.0 was giving us, I was exactly in the same situation. I wanted her hardly, even if I had other girls, plus I always liked her and now that I could have her, my goal was just there. And she was giving the idea to be quite hot under the sheets. Keeping communicating with her the whole morning, I was still asking myself if I would have broken the rules or not. Lately, I promised myself to be less rational and more instinctive. During the last break I spoke with John about it. As a friend and a male he understood me very well. At the end, using a known expression that I myself had invented and that I often used, he simply said: "Gas!". I was breaking the rules of the Test but I was aware of one thing: this experiment originated to give us answers that helped us to improve our relationship with the other sex. Now that we had some more answers and more results, it would have been crazy not to capitalize. I decided that the following day I would have proposed to the fantastic four to bring this change: from now on, thanks to the new mentality, if some guy had had the occasion, he could have had sex with a chick. According to the initial philosophy of the Test, this would have been a contradiction but up to the new awareness it was not. Initially we had deprived the guys of the possibility to approach the girls to see what would have happened. Now that we had a better way to approach the girls which made us appear more attractive and granted us more success, it made sense to capitalize up to the end. Although the Test was not ended yet, old times when we were chasing after girls were over. It was right to gratify ourselves. I thought that this could have meant the end of the Test: if the guys could now go further with girls, the Test itself actually didn't exist anymore. This doubt stopped me for a second and I decided to postpone the proposal to the next day. I had to think about it....and fuck Ilary. According to my new proposal to be less rational and more instinctive, I chose to go to Ilary's that afternoon. Coming out of school I met Tiffany near my scooter: her being short together with her thin figure was driving me crazy. I didn't even have time to agree with Ilary about the afternoon that another one was going around me. There were remote possibilities to sleep with Tiffany because she was young but as a paradox it was better this way. As soon as I got to my Vespa she said right away. "I loved it this morning during the break..." leaving the sentence hanging. Then she said: "We could go to the park, this afternoon...". "Damn I could take her with me to Ilary's to make thing even juicier." I thought with a light smile on my face. I had agreed with Ilary to meet at five at her place. It was only 12,30 so I could make the Combo. "I think you could be cold in the park this afternoon..." I answered not accepting her plans immediately. She answered. "You could warm me up..." "What about going to my place?" Stating more than asking. I think she was so in love, that, even if she knew her mother would have bothered her, she said yes. "It was about time!" I thought with a shiver of self esteem that crossed my body. She sat on my Vespa and we headed it to my place. From lunch to dinner the house was completely free. I prepared lunch just to show that I could cook, even if we just had a plate of pasta. Compared to the other times we've been together, that afternoon we could speak a little bit more and get to know each other better. I realized that she wanted to see me also and overall for this reason: after all I like it too. We realized with had a lot in common but, on other sides, we were deeply different: the funny thing was that she liked football and I didn't. It was rather amusing listening to Tiffany speaking about the championship as if she was a sport anchorwoman. As my old friend Steve had taught me I turned the heat up, just to facilitate Tifffany's physical involvement. She would have taken off her clothes easier. Quickly the atmosphere got hotter and we stated kissing passionately for a long time. As I already thought I wouldn't go further with her but it was ok: respecting the Test rules (to break them with Ilary was more than enough) and now, having all these chances I didn't need anything more. And I understood that this feeling of not continuos need was paradoxically the cause and not the consequence. In the past I would have told myself that I could have felt this way only after getting certain results. Actually results weren't generating this feeling in me but exactly the other way around! Understanding and accept this concept was a good result. It had started to make an incredible difference.

Believing in yourself more transmitted a more strong and attractive image which led to results that increased this virtuous circle. But actually, the beginning of this winning path was represented by what I felt and not by results that we couldn't reach if we didn't start with the right approach. In other words, the common belief that just getting to a certain objective could have made you feel in a certain way wasn't correct. If you wanted to reach your goal, you should have felt as if you had already reached it. We often believe that a certain mental approach is the consequence of our situations but now I deeply believed the contrary. You should have generated the desired situation and reality after would have tuned with your deep state of mind. Now that I felt stronger in the relationship with girls, I was obtaining results that I have never seen before in the entire school year. It was incredible that I was thinking like this in spite of the high physical and emotional involvement with Tiffany: and it was not the first time. We let ourselves dragged along into an overflowing physical attraction until four o' clock when I decided to stop to have time for Ilary. Even this was incredible, as for my parameters: in the past I would have never stopped a girl from kissing me. Now I had got so much self esteem to decide to do so. The "old Luke" would have said: "Of course you can do it because you have Ilary waiting for you at home". But now I understood that the concept was upside down. Ilary was waiting for me just because I felt first of all that I could do it. In other words my new self esteem and over all self consciousness allowed me to obtain results that I would have only imagined in the past. Feeling this new self esteem and stopping the continuous fear for my performances in all situations, I was living a period extremely full of positive experiences. I took Tiffany back home, leaving her one hundred meters from the entrance to avoid that her mother could see us. We said bye with an intense and very long kiss. We fixed a date for the following day at school, at the break time (she wanted to meet at eight but I explained that for me it was impossible to arrive at school that early). Tiffany went in and while I was ready to leave to go towards Ilary's house, I received a text from Chiara, Giulia's friend. It was a rather confused text: she said that she was feeling something for me but at the same time she didn't want to interfere between me and Giulia, her best friend. Nothing else. I didn't know what to answer and considering I was late, as usual, I did not reply. I got on my Vespa heading towards Ilary's. I arrived there unusually on time. She opened the door smiling and I noticed her casual T-shirt that showed to be very easy and quick to take off. We spoke a little bit of our class teasing the grinds and then we got to the point: just like some hours earlier, the situation warmed up quickly. Compared to Tiffany, Ilary had surely more experience: I felt she was sure of herself and fully aware of what she wanted. We were already naked in her bed when we heard the door downstairs opening: it was her brother that was coming in with his girlfriend. Ilary didn't expect it and for a moment we stopped and remained silent. Her brother's bedroom was near to hers but we heard that the two lovers remained downstairs, in the living room. Grateful to them, we continued our hot effusions. I understood only now how sexy Ilary was. While making love, Ilary moaning with pleasure and I heard her brother's voice that from downstairs asked: "Ilary, is that you?" and Ilary, promptly answered with a convinced "Yes!". I almost broke down laughing in that crazy situation. At the end we kept talking as we did the first time we kissed in the park. I felt things between us were getting intimate and that her interest towards me was more intense. I don't know if this was good or not. Then I went to the bathroom and when I was getting out wearing just a pair of boxers, I met Ilary brother's girlfriend (not bad at all). She smiled and said hello. Back to Ilary's room, we started talking of Saturday's party: I clearly felt she absolutely wanted me to go with her. I neither confirm nor refuse, just to keep her in suspense and increase her desire for me. Plus I wanted to be free that night, without having to stay with her all night long. Considering my lasts results, It didn't make sense binding myself to one girl, even just for one night. So I didn't give her a definitive answer and I left her to go home. On my way, listening loudly to my song "Get Down" in my headphones, I felt that wonderful sensation I felt the day before. It was a great period, full of successes with girls. And I was fully enjoying it. When I got home, I had dinner and I spent the evening at home without any dramatic event: I just chatted on facebook. Suddenly I took my iPhone and I went through Chiara's message again. It was a confused message but I could understand she was feeling something for me but at the same time she didn't want Giulia to know. I knew what she was talking about. I didn't want to make Giulia suffer as well but Chiara was a hot chick and, considering the period, I couldn't stop results I was obtaining. This is more or less what I answered her and she replied in less than one minute. "Hey, she had her telephone in her hands, she was so quick!". I thought. The summer before we had a good time together and I wasn't dating Giulia yet. We kept our secret, anyway because we didn't think it could have been important since no one of the three of us was in a relation. After a while I started dating Giulia and Chiara's hopes started falling. Now that Giulia and I were in a "thinking" period, Chiara took advantage of it to make a little step forward trying to respect her friend at the same time. She was probably pushing herself a little to much further considering that even if Giulia and I weren't officially dating we were about to. My fervent imagination started bringing me to daydream (or maybe it never stopped) about hot games with Chiara and Giulia together with me. In the past I would have excluded things like these from the very beginning but now after the "the new Luke" was born, I even believed it could have happened. After all neither Giulia nor Chiara were so "slow" so maybe one day my dream could have come true. A blond and a brunette, sexy and irresistible together with me in bed....I couldn't ask for more! She wrote me she wanted to see me and talk about this situation now that Giulia and I weren't back together: I could understand her and I thought it was better to talk now and not when Giulia and I would have bee dating again. I told her we could have met in the pub near my house in half an hour. She answered yes so I started getting ready. In that moment, I thought "old John" would have told me the important thing. I wondered what it could have been. I got to the pub and I saw her near the entrance, wearing a wool hat covering her long beautiful blond hair. I walked to her fiercely, curious to know how the night would have turned. At this point I could expect everything to happen. "Hi thank you for coming.", She began. "Hi, don't worry...are you ok?" I promptly answered. "Oh yes, everything ok, do you want to get in?" She asked impatiently. We went inside the pub that was pretty crowded despite the working day. We sat down in a little table for two. I remember that sitting next to her I could smell that good perfume which was taking me back to many nice moments of the past. Chiara was very pretty, nice and friendly. If I didn't meet Giulia I would have probably gone out with Chiara and who knows what it would have happened. The waiter came to our table and we ordered a tea for her and the usual Guinness for me. The atmosphere between us was quite relaxing and enjoyable and I was a little surprised considering what we have lived in the past and considering that we were there to talk about the whole situation. We joked a little just to get comfortable and then she said: "You know Luke, you're dating my best friend and the last thing I want is to hurt her. I wouldn't hurt anybody in the world, I can't imagine hurting Giuly". I felt her close to me and clear. We had fun together in the past but our relation didn't grew as it did with Giulia. Chiara started feeling something deep for me only after I started dating Giulia. She kept on talking: "At the same time, I realize I feel something for you, something deep which never changed despite the fact that you started dating my best friend. During whole this time, I tried not to think about it, trying to address my thought somewhere else but I could't make it. Until you will be with her, I will see you often and this will not help me." Honestly, I was very moved. By her words but mainly by her non verbal language, I could clearly understand that what she felt for me was far more what I imagined. I have thought it was just a crash on me due to the fact that she could not have me and this was increasing her attraction. The usual desire to get what you can't have but I was wrong. So wrong. "Maybe you didn't get it or maybe you did, anyway every time I see you in school or when you are with Giulia I wish you were mine. And feel guilty because my dream clashes with my love for my best friend. This confuses me and makes me sad, after all." I thought the situation was more complicated than what I've thought. Chiara wasn't happy because she couldn't be with me and at the same time she felt as she was a bad friend because she wanted her best friend's guy. No doubt, this was a mess. I was feeling an attraction toward Chiara which went beyond the pure physical push. She was similar to Giulia for many aspects but very different in another way, with a complexity that made her interesting and attractive. I didn't want to hurt Giulia either and I wished to make the situation clear for everyone. But I slowly understood this was impossible. I couldn't make her stop talking so I let her finish without interrupting. "I know you and Giulia aren't seeing each other now but I know Giuly wants to go back with you and she wants it badly. When we talk about it I feel a contrast in me: on one hand, as a friend, I'm happy for you two getting back together but on the other hand a part of me knows that if you're not going to get beck together, I will have more chances to be happy....with you". The whole situation was far more complicated than what I expected....a mess, I would say. "I took this "hanging" period between you two, to talk to you and tell you what I feel and hear what you think..." I realized in that moment that she was opening up and making herself vulnerable, telling me exactly what she was feeling for me. She had risked a lot and for this reason I admired her. It is not simple to open up sharing the most intimate and hidden parts of ourselves. I tried to answer extremely kindly and in the most delicate way. Since she had opened herself up, I decided to be honest and sincere. After all, I think that as risky and difficult it can be, it is important to open up to others if you really want to feel the depth of a relationship which can help during our lifetime. "You know Chiara, I appreciate your honesty and opening and realize that it is not easy at all to come here and tell me everything you have told me, even more so when your best friend is involved."

She smiled: "Thanks to have understood without judging." I kept on: "As you, the last thing I would do is hurting Giulia. That's why we have taken a break: she left me because she was living a hard period when her parents seemed to separate and now, just a few days ago, she asked me to get back together. I haven't given her an answer yet because I wanted to think about it myself too." She stopped me showing surprise: "Giuly told me that you would have got back together in a short time." She asked me the other day but I have not answered yet. It's clear she firmly hopes so." Chiara immediately replied: "You have doubts?" I smiled for her question so intimate: "I want to do the right thing." I answered vaguely and I continued: "I think I changed a lot lately, overall, in my relation with girls and I'm thinking about my relationship with Giulia. I was very hurt when she left me and I wished I could have gone back with her as soon as possible. Now that she's the one that is asking me, I'm the one that takes time in giving an answer. Isn't life ironic...? I feel that I made steps forward in the meanwhile which have taken me to a new awareness." I realized that it would have been difficult for Chiara to understand deeply what I meant. I didn't feel like talking about my latest "relations" and I couldn't absolutely mention the Test. "In a short time I will give Giulia an answer but in the meanwhile I want to be sure that I think about it deeply in order to make the right choice. A part of me wants to get back together but another side want to go further to try new experiences. My situation is not less messy than yours." I said hoping to make her smile. I honestly hoped that she could understand me. After all we both were, actually the three of us, in a rather difficult situation. It was very improbable to be able to find a solution that could please everybody. I've always been 'diplomatic', careful to make everybody happy, avoiding conflicts at all costs. Unfortunately situations can't be solved in a peaceful and easy way all the time. In this case, inevitably, somebody would get hurt. "Honestly Chiara, I like you. I've always liked you. Something about you really attracts me, you are tremendously attractive to my eyes." I told her this shamelessly. It was time to show one's feelings and be honest. She had opened herself up to me and it was right that I did the same to her. I saw her face brighten up and her posture became firmer. To make her happy even just for a moment gave me pleasure, but it would have been just a moment, that's all. And it was important not to trick her with false hopes. I let myself go and told her with an open heart what I was feeling too: "You have an incredible face and magnetic eyes which make you look like a modern version of Grace Kelly. Your perfume is exciting and it makes me remember the wonderful moments spent together...." She looked surprised. I don't think she expected these compliments from me; she hoped maybe, but surely did not expect them. "You really think so?" She asked with a light and very sweet voice. I knew that hope was increasing inside her: unluckily this was developing also the illusion on her part of starting something between us again.

Something that was beyond simple words. Considering how things were going lately nothing could be excluded. "Yes, it's like that" I answered with decision.

"I'm torn between the respect for Giulia and the desire of letting free passion express itself freely. If you and I let ourselves go I think it could have had devastating consequences in my relation with Giulia and in your friendship with her." I realized that I was going too far, meaning something intimate between us. I saw Chiara getting closer saying in a low voice: "Certain passions can't be stopped and if we feel something, it's right to express it...." I felt my attraction for her increasing beyond measure. The atmosphere was warming up and having opened our deep feelings to each other had drawn us closer. Literally.

The risk of passing the limit of "no return" was high. The attraction was evident and increasing more and more while each of us expressed freely his feelings.

We were both fighting between the idea of being "friends", which wouldn't satisfy none of us but would save our relation with Giulia or letting ourselves go without thinking. After all we were just adolescents. I could feel this conflict on her part about "what to do" which was going on for too long: The fact that I had told her about my attraction for her, complicated things even more. At tis point it was almost natural to give free play to our impulses: the easiest thing to do but so dangerous for the consequences. Honestly I didn't feel to deceive my relation with Giulia and I felt that Chiara respected her best friend deeply. Chiara went to the bathroom so I had some time to think. In the last period I had decided to be less rational and more instinctive but in this case the old Luke seemed to prevail. Chiara came back to the table and we ordered more drinks. This time she ordered a Long Island. We started being rather high. At twelve thirty we got up, left the table and went out of the pub. The attraction had been high all night, this together with some drinks created a fatal mix. When out, I took her to her scooter where it was clear by now that we would have kissed. Something that simply couldn't stop. Our instinct prevailed on all the words and talking said before. It was an incredibly pleasant kiss, long and intimate. After so long, it was really great to feel again Chiara's taste. We stayed there near the scooter for an endless time; it was evident that we both had been looking for that moment for so long and now we were enjoying it.

We let passion go, we regained our composure and said bye without adding a word. With after wit I wasn't surprised of how the night ended: Chiara showed her interest and I encouraged her telling her that I was attracted to her too. Conclusions were already written. I went to bed not thinking about it too much and I slept till morning.

CHAPTER 14

THE SPONTANEOUS
EVOLUTION OF THE TEST

Thursday, October the 13rd

The day after I got to school unusually early and I realized that John had
to tell me the latest news. I went to him enthusiastic wishing to know what
was going to happen. He told me to wait for the break so that he could
gather all our friends. I couldn't wait. Anyway, during the lessons Ilary,
with who I had fun the day before, was sitting in front of me so that I could
look at her cute butt and nicely get to the morning break. I was grateful
to her for this reason. It was finally time for the break and I run with John
in the courtyard ready to enjoy the already anticipated new: we gathered
the Magnificent 4 plus a few other guys from other classes. I thought that
if someone had seen us, we were looking as a serious business group: the
organization and the accuracy were incredible. And the girls didn't know
anything. After all, how could anyone thing about the experiment we have
put together! I already told John that talking in the courtyard was too risky
but we kept on. He started enjoying risking as I did and we were so sure of
ourselves that we didn't care that much. As in the beginning of the Test,
the excitement was high and we were really happy to share our opinions
on the development of the Test we were living. All the guys were listening
to John who started speaking using his incredible dialectics:

"As you all know, the first part of the Test helped us to understand a
series of dynamics between girls and boys which led us to an improvement
and to deeper consciousness. As a consequence, even the results improved.

The project was born as a joke and a provocation that could help us understanding how to relate to girls in a more effective way.

In the beginning the rules forced us to adopt a new behavior compared to the one we were used to; a behavior that forced us, without being aware, not to do certain things we were used to do. Without the experiment, we would have never act differently, all of us with all the girls. The coincidence of all these new factors helped us to review what we have been thinking could be possible or effective with girls. We couldn't chase after girls and at the same time we could only have a simple friendship with them and this is why we seemed more attractive to them. We understood this only later. Results initially improved and we were extremely astonished: now we understand why and it's a lesson that will help us to improve. In a second phase we noticed how this friendship attitude towards girls caused an opposite effect after a period in which girls started getting closer like they never did before. Here again, we've understood later that a more secure and detached attitude gives a better result in the beginning but it can't be enough to establish a satisfying and effective relationship with girls. At this point the phase number two of Test has started, when, even keeping unchanged the spirit and the objective of the project, we've introduced the possibility for the guys of getting up to kissing. This allowed us to have more points of reflection for further improvement. As a matter of fact, if we hadn't introduced this change, we wouldn't have obtained any significant result.

An easier and more secure approach can work in the beginning of an interaction with a girl but just to build a starting connection. Afterwards it's necessary to have the support of a strategy which is functional to the objective. Just to find out and test these strategies, we've decided to allow the guys to get up to kissing in order to get deeper in the relation with the girls. Today we see that the new type of approach deriving from the awareness obtained by the first part of the Test is helping us and, together with the fact of being able to get to the point, it's giving great results."

All the guys, including me, nodded looking at each other agreeing with what John was saying. John kept on resolutely: "Just like in the first part of the Test we had a phase of immobility due to the fact that the girls got tired of our lack of interest, even now I think it can happen, and in some cases it has already happened, that the girls (and the guys) will desire to go far beyond kissing. If this won't happen, even if we've learnt an important lesson, we'll be again in a situation where we could not go deeper to get the results deserved. To make it simple, it could be time to loosen up the belt and give more freedom to the guys to capitalize on the new consciousness. If we do this before a new phase of immobility, we could get to the end of the Test with a better and higher awareness, a better approach and excellent results. If we don't do it, we could waste and ruin good potentialities." Actually this was exactly what I myself had recently thought but had not told John yet. Obviously, I agreed with him. As a matter of fact once again I had anticipated the changes of the Test, not to say that I had broken the rules. When John ended his speech, Jack asked immediately: "Does this mean that the guys are allowed to get up to 'under the sheet' with girls?" John answered concisely: "Precisely." To make the atmosphere lighter, I said: "My goodness, couldn't you tell us right away, instead of going through this speech?" There was a general laughter that I stopped immediately and said: "Obviously I am joking. What you said up to now summarizes perfectly the evolution of the Test and I like the idea of learning from what has happened and so anticipate eventual future changes. In other words make the rules less strict not to be in a blind alley like in the first part of the Test: the girls not considering us." I felt that the general mood was high and there was an implicit agreement on what I and John had said up to now. I thought how I had already broken the rules myself in the first part of the Test anticipating its evolution. Therefore even in this case, with a little change, my behavior would be legalized. One of the guys interrupted my thought expressing a doubt: "By doing this, won't we actually consider the Test over? By having all freedom of doing everything with the girls it's like considering the Test finished." The question was interesting and correct. John answered promptly: "Actually by doing so, it is as if the Test itself came to an end. But it wouldn't necessarily be a tragedy: this experiment had started to supply us with responses. We've already got a lot and I think that if we don't change the rules, we might not have any new ones and not capitalize on what we learnt. Therefore if the Test had to finish technically, we would be anyway in the situation of being able to keep learning with better awareness this time. It's almost as if the Test, as a paradox, should end in order to keep carrying on its functions in helping us to grow in this field." I think everything was perfectly clear. The Test was just a mean with the aim of supporting us all in the growth and better comprehension of the relationship with girls. If the rules now limited somehow these aims, it was right to modify them. We took sometime before deciding what to do and agreed on thinking about it for a few days before making a definite choice. The bell rang loudly and that meant that we had to sadly go back into our classrooms. When I entered my classroom I found out that the fourth hour was free since the teacher was sick. I spent the whole time talking to Ilary until I received a sms from Giulia stating she wanted to speak to me as soon as possible. I had a weird sensation that she had found out about my date and following kissing with Chiara. I decided to send a message to Chiara to invite her to meet in the corridor immediately to speak about the issue. She had physical training but she skipped it and therefore free to meet me. I went out of the classroom and reached the meeting point, at the snack distributor on the first floor. I was ready to talk about Giulia's message but as soon as I saw her, still emotioned for the recent kiss, I felt a very strong attraction for her. Chiara herself thought I had called her just to meet and not to speak of Giulia's message. We said very few words. "Hi Luke! How are you?" She said with enthusiasm. "Hi, everything is great or almost....."I answered, as to anticipate the impression I had of Giulia's message. While speaking, I could clearly smell her perfume and that was literally weakening my inhibitors. I was afraid I knew how it would end. "Something wrong"? She asked: "Well, I got a message from Giulia. She wants to talk to me..." "I see. I haven't told her anything about us of course, so I don't think we should worry." "I understand and...." Chiara interrupted me immediately: "Anyway I am very undecided if I should tell her or not. Giuly is my best friend and even if you are not dating her at the moment, I don't think that what I did is fair to her." Inside I could understand her but it was evident that to say everything to Giulia could have dangerous consequences. To find out that her best friend and her boyfriend had a date and kissing surely couldn't please her so much. We had taken a break to think, that's true, but the fact of going out with her best friend wasn't something that she would take lightly. "Do you think that the best thing is just telling her?" I asked cold blooded. "I don't know. I can't pretend that nothing has happened. I'll see her this afternoon as well. What should I do? Should I say nothing at all"? I answered promptly: "If you tell her everything she will feel very bad. You know Giulia is very sensitive." Chiara added: "Well, after all we just kissed and if I confess it, I know she will forgive me. I think it's the best solution". As soon as she pronounced these words she came closer and changed her tone of voice: "or would you rather keep it secret?" She asked with a nasty tone of voice. The mix of emotions in that moment was really tremendous. In the beginning, as soon as I met her near the food distributor, just the sight of her had caused me a strong desire of jumping on her. Then I felt to just inform her of the message and I was concerned of how to handle the situation. Now the simple attraction was overwhelming again and prevailing over words and worries. Thousands of thoughts in my mind that tried to justify that what I was doing was not wrong. Chiara just like me was troubled. On one side she felt strongly her friendship for Giulia and respect but on the other hand she was at the mercy of her instinct which suggested to let herself go. The first of us to succumb to emotions would have started what was easy to predict. We were now very close physically while speaking which let imagined nothing good or maybe something good, it depended on the points of view. I, once again, brought back to my mind the agreement I had with myself: being less rational and more instinctive. In this case this meant kissing Chiara in the corridor caring less of the consequences. Probably it would have been the right thing to do and surely the most pleasant one. I felt a certain connection with Chiara in that moment almost as if she felt the same I did for every change of emotion of mine. When she came even closer while we were speaking, even trying to hold back, an invisible force was pushing us towards each other. While we were speaking, overwhelmed by pure attraction, we kissed intensely and passionately. If a moment before we had held back our emotions, now the flow of our feelings overwhelmed the borders of rationality and hit us with incredible force. We enjoyed that moment more than the first time we kissed. It was powerful and incredibly pleasant. We withdrew in a corner of the corridor and kept on for long minutes. After so many words, finally we were doing what we both were feeling. I finally could really feel Chiara's body and I realized how thin and tonic she was: this increased my desire and pleasure. I could feel her emotion and attraction that could have ended to something more serious. Even if we were in school. In fact the conclusion seemed to be that. We withdrew inside a store room used by janitors and started to take off our clothes. In this moment, in an escalation of passion, Chiara stopped me with decision even if she was fighting with herself:

"I cannot, I really can't!" She said recomposing herself. "What?" I answered with surprise. "I cannot do this to Giuly, I don't want." She repeated it more firmly. As soon as I heard these words I thought about Giulia's sweet face and my rational part prevailed. Even if what we were doing was incredibly pleasant, I understood that if Giulia had known she would feel very bad. Besides I know that we couldn't make it not to tell her. We put our clothes back on and left the store room. Unbelievable to realize how we were so excited a few minutes before while now everything was over all of a sudden. I told myself it was better this way. Even if we didn't have a relation, Giulia didn't deserve to be hurt. Even if this meant to hide to myself my feelings for Chiara. It was probably the right thing to do, or that was my way of thinking at the moment. Before saying bye to Chiara and going back to the class, I tried to understand how to handle the issue with Giulia: she had to go back to the gym immediately therefore we agreed about meeting in the afternoon. She had to meet Giulia but she would have find the time to discuss the situation. I ran back to my class but there was no lesson and no substitute teaching. Totally free. Better this way since I had spent so long time out. I sat down and replied to Giulia's text stating that we could meet in the afternoon: I was really interested in hearing what she had to say. More than likely she didn't know anything about my flirting with Chiara and she simply desired to talk about our relation: even so, I still needed to speak to Chiara to handle the situation. The fourth hour of school was almost over so I spent the last minutes talking to Ilary: usually I didn't find very interesting to talk to the girls, I rather preferred their physical look, the best way to share my emotions with them. Nevertheless, the dialogue was pleasant and amusing with her, full of flashes about our recent good moments together. I really enjoyed that. I understood that she could date me for a while if I agreed but there were several variables to analyze: first of all I had already broken the rules by sleeping with her and I would break them again if I had done it again (even if, after John's speech, I was sure that the rules would change soon). I needed to think of how the 'menage a trois' with Giulia and Chiara could be handled, and last but not least I couldn't forget Tiffany since I still desired to see her. Too many things to think about or maybe too much 'thinking'. While these thoughts were filling my mind, my attention steered towards Ilary who asked me to meet in those days. I said I was very busy and that I would get back to her later on. As usually, by showing little interest I surely would have gained more interest to her and over all I would have understood the way of handling the latest news. Undoubtedly, thanks to the Test, these last weeks were the most intense and unpredictable of the last months or even years. I couldn't but realize that this was due to the radical changes brought which had obliged me to come out of my 'comfort zone': in the past, too often I was limited and closed in habits that made my life too predictable and that kept me from expressing the potential that only now know to have. Facing my fears in the way I was doing in these weeks was certainly the hardest thing but surely the most rewarding as well. I had obtained so many good results in my relationship with girls that I found myself in the situation of having to postpone dating. Enough to give an idea of how much I was changing. The sound of the bell interrupted my thoughts and brought me back to reality. I spent the last hour of school chatting on Facebook with Tiffany that I really desired seeing. She gave me an appointment outside near my Vespa. If we had changed the rules of the Test allowing the possibility of sleeping with the girls, I could have fun with her and that was very exciting. Lost in my thoughts and chatting with Tiffany, the last hour of school flew away and in no time the bell rang finally announcing my freedom. I went down to the courtyard where I saw Chiara speaking to some class mates, friends with Giulia as well. They were looking at me so I decided to stop and chat with them a bit: they were all very nice girls but Camilla stood out with her very sweet face and her long, brown and curly hair. She had a perfume that was similar to Giulia's and I liked that very much. In that moment I felt that if I wanted I could have started dating her and know her better. I guess my new self esteem in the relation with girls was giving me this easy attitude in approaching them. Now, like never before, I realized how much this project had helped me to bring out potential and talent that I didn't even think I had and this sensation was just wonderful! Hardly realizing it, my personal growth of these last weeks had allowed me to bring out skills for too long unknown and develop winning strategies with girls. All this happened without any plan or expectations. Simply extraordinary!

Although I had to settle a few things on which I had given some deep thought while I was at school and Ilary had asked me to see each other, the idea of Camilla was temping me. Once again my instinct showed clearly the way to follow and thanks to the great improvements of the last period, I was now able to undertake successfully any direction chosen. Not only was I aware of what I had to do in any moment of my life but also I had the capacity of following any new path with trust and courage. Considering the short time in which this had happened, all this was even more astonishing and stimulating. In any moment I could see clearly the right choice to make and I suppose that in the past, deep inside, I always knew the right thing to do: I simply did not see it clearly. Or rather didn't want to see it. Now I had gained more clearness and courage. I had changed a lot or maybe for the first time in my life I was really myself. In a few weeks I had gone a long way far from my old self and I had reached a new consideration of myself which was probably the most real one. Now I felt more free and I was finally holding the reins of my life in my hands. Everything was so strong. In the optics of this new Luke, while in the past I never would have thought to enlarge my chances undertaking new directions, now I was asking myself: "Why not?". Thinking about Camilla this strong question was pushing me to a deeper interest towards her. "Hi, Luke!" Chiara said, standing out with her black leggins that underlined her thin and tonic legs. "Hi, girls, are you charged up for tomorrow night?" I asked trying to keep the general energy high. The following night a private birthday party was organized by a girl from the fourth grade. I looked forward to seeing how things would go considering that the rules of the Test were still valid. More than likely it could have been a great occasion to push us to change the rules before Friday. Expecting a good behavior from all those guys was unreal and I myself wanted to feel free to enjoy myself. Moreover this was a particular party where all the guests would wear pajamas: it was a pajamas party with guys and girls that from 9.30 would go wild with the sound of loud house music and drinking from the open bar. A very promising prelude. We had absolutely to change the rules, I thought smiling. It was just Camilla that answered to my question: "We are certainly charged up for tomorrow night, what about you, who are you coming with?" "I'll be there with my usual clan of friends in mission: John, Jack and the others. We'll have a lot of work to do!" I answered jokingly without specifying that we had deep interest for the girls of the first and second grade. "Work? What does that mean?" Chiara asked. John had invented this word to mean our playing with girls. "Oh... nothing." I cut it short. I thought that Tiffany was waiting near my scooter so I decided to leave the group to go towards my Vespa. I decided anyway to hit on Camilla: what I recently understood was that anytime my intuition told me something, I should have immediately and quickly done something before fear and excuses rose. Getting to the parking, I could see Tiffany sitting on my Vespa, waiting for me. I heard a voice that I new screaming from my backs: "Luke, wait!" It was Chiara that left her friends running to tell me something privately. "Luke, don't forget that we have to meet each other this afternoon, it's important!" "Sure!" I answered. "Ok, then, see you later." She said kissing me, quickly but sweetly. I kept not understanding what she wanted to do. Her friendship with Giulia kept her that same morning from having sex with me but at the same time she was keeping showing a great interest for me, even physically. I told her goodbye and went to Tiffany still thinking about this.

CHAPTER 15

HOW COULD SOMETHING THAT GIVES YOU PLEASURE, BE WRONG?

"Hi babe!" I exclaimed as if we were together. "Hi little Luke, how are you?" She replied in a tender way. "I'm alright, been waiting long?" I responded. "Nah, don't worry. Where are we headed now?" She asked with a voice wrapped with pure curiosity. She was giving me full freedom of act so I decided to go for lunch to a close by pizzeria to see how the first part of the afternoon would develop. Nevertheless the remaining time was limited because I should have met with Chiara and Giulia as well. For a moment even the theory that every now and then I should have studied crossed my mind but I laughed about it, thinking that in that period I had more important and enjoyable things to do.

I cranked up my Vespa and Tiffany hopped on, hugging me with her delicate arms. I headed towards the pizzeria where we would have eaten something for lunch. Despite the speed, I was able to smell her perfume that was driving me crazy; as soon as we got to the pizzeria I made good use of the moment and kissed her again to taste her once more. We had a pizza and so I decided to take her to my place. After all she had technically given me carte blanche. Once there I immediately realized she wanted to have some fun as much as I wanted to and that was making me dangerously excited. We went upstairs to my room and we started kissing with an incredible intensity; I have always thought that the rules in this case wouldn't be an issue because with her being young, I would have never made it under the bed sheets. But now I felt that the objective was within reach and I was partially torn. I had already broken the rules in the first part of the Test and in the second one I didn't want do indulge in such behavior. However as easily predictable, passion and pure attraction overcame us and we ended up doing it for real, on my big queen size bed.

It was incredibly pleasant. As I imagined. It was as if she had been expecting this moment for long time and somehow I had finally reached my goal. After doing it, we kept talking a bit until I noticed it was incredibly late and that I wasn't on time for my date with Chiara and Giulia. I grabbed my iPhone and noticed 2 missed calls, one from Chiara and one from Giulia. I gave one last bite to Tiffany's solid arse and I took her back home in no time. I finally headed to Giulia's and as soon as I got there, I saw what resembled Chiara's scooter there. I had a strange feeling. I went up and when I entered Chiara's house they were both in front of me; I didn't know what Giulia knew, whether Chiara had told her anything or how things actually were. I felt some tension in the air and I saw that Giulia's face was quite grim. I didn't know whether I should have played dead or if I had to prove myself unrelated from the situation, or what.

I should have talked to Chiara alone beforehand, to see how to manage this.

"Chiara told me everything..." Giulia muttered, giving an end to all my doubts. I thought Chiara hadn't been able to keep the secret. "Everything what?" I replied in a not convincing and probably stupid way. "...that you two kissed, more than once..." She asserted with an extremely disappointed voice. I saw Chiara totally different from after school: she was sad and she was giving the idea of being very sorry. Of course it wasn't fun for her to tell Giulia everything and she could have certainly told me something before it happened, nevertheless I got the picture. I tried to contain the harm, trying not to hurt Giulia as much as possible. "Yes, it's true, it happened." I bravely asserted without hiding anything. Since Chiara confessed and since I didn't want to cause additional pain to Giulia, I went for the hard and naked truth. "...and I can tell you that I'm really sorry if this makes you feel sad..." I added right away. I thought that admitting and honestly saying that I was sorry, as I really was, was the best thing to do. I really cared for Giulia and despite the crush for Chiara, she had always been my favourite. I felt for her what I had never felt for anyone else and maybe I realised that I had never really showed that. I saw Giulia's face sad and disappointed as ever; I generally knew that when she was sad she used to withdraw into herself and not communicate with anybody. That time was no exception. "How could you Luke?" She mercilessly asked, making me honestly feel like shit. After all it was only a kiss, actually two, but I must admit that if it wasn't for Chiara, I would have gone further. For the first time in the last two weeks I questioned the fact that following mostly your instinct instead of logic was the right thing to do. Maybe in this case I should have listened more to the old Luke but how could something that gave me so much pleasure, be wrong?" Those strange reflections that were resulting in philosophy flashed through my head as I was about to answer to Giulia. "I'm sorry, really. In this period we are not together and it simply happened..." I replied trying to make her understand that it was something meaningless even if in deep I felt something for Chiara. "So it happened? Then you know what? That you and your date can even leave my house, now!" Chiara and I left the house noticeably worried and sorry. I think that none of the two of us had never seen Giulia so mad and disappointed at the same time. We arrived in the courtyard and I immediately started pressing Chiara: "Why didn't you wait for me? Didn't we have to meet to clarify all this?" I firmly asked. "I came to Giuly's and I think that, I don't know how, she had already grasped it and it was impossible for me to keep the secret. At that point it was better to tell her the truth. I was already feeling guilty enough. And now it's even worse!" "Yeah but we had to meet beforehand to decide how to manage all this. Now Giulia took it so badly, she didn't even give me a chance to talk and we both ended up looking like jerks!" Chiara replied: "Well it's late now. I'll see what I can do to make her feel better, I'm really really sorry for poor Giuly. Shit!" "I hear you!" I said. "It's all a fucking mess." I added. I felt that if Chiara and I had spoken before meeting with Giulia we could have limited the damage. Nevertheless I didn't feel like arguing with her so I rather decided to think about how to solve it or at least how to talk to Giulia. I hopped on my Vespa and I headed home, hunting for reflections. Chiara, I don't know why, was on foot so I had to give her a lift. Clearly, the scooter I saw when I got to Giulia's wasn't hers. I dropped her at her place and we decided that we would have kept in touch to see how to manage the situation properly. We both wanted Giulia to understand that we were sorry, and also since her parents almost broke up, she didn't deserve to suffer in any way. I arrived home and I laid down on the bed trying to think about the situation. In no time I got a message from Giulia herself. She was really disappointed and sad, especially because I went with her best friend. I replied I was sorry and that after all what happened had no meaning. She didn't reply anymore. Besides, I found John online on Facebook and we had a little chat. He reaffirmed what he had told me the last time when we were in the courtyard with the other guys. The rules had to be changed before a new stall phase arrived that prevented any new improvement. Furthermore that the sleepover party was coming up. I didn't tell him that I had already broken the rules and that now I had a big problem to solve. I only told him that I agreed we needed to change the rules even if technically that would mean the end of the Test: after all we were only interested in answers and personal improvement. But until today things went pretty well and it was fundamental to go on the same way. Finally allowing the boys to make it under the bed sheets, we would have permitted anybody to capitalise the work already done, obtaining at the same time many additional answers regarding relation with the opposite sex. As in fact we had already noticed and expressed, this Test was born to answer a provocative question but honestly we didn't know what to expect. Of course we would never imagine that we would have made it up to the point that the whole project would have turned into a growth and improvement project for every guy in school. It was certainly a result that went far beyond our greatest expectations and that also gives a noble touch to the cause: from a simple odd idea, it changed to something that helped and was helping several guys. And this, I think, gave us honour. But even more, it gave honour to all the people in school that put effort for the success of the project, respecting the rules and taking the best in term of results. Now the next step could be to allow everyone that had already showed reliability and commitment, to go all the way with the girls they were dating: the time was ripe. As I was saying goodbye to John, telling him I would see him the following day at school, where we would continue our chat, I got a message from Giulia, replying my message she hadn't replied before. She was telling me she didn't know if she could forgive me because of what had happened and after all I could understand her. I thought I should have given her some time to make her ponder and allow her to get over her initial discouragement. Then I would have approached her to try to fix the damage and put our relationship back together. At this point I was terribly craving to get back with her and the mistake I made with Chiara made me understand what I really felt. Strange how sometimes it was necessary to make some mistakes that even if pleasant, allowed us to see what the right path to cross was. As much as I didn't want to deny the fact that what happened with Chiara was incredibly enjoyable, I realised that the right girl was Giulia; after all I always knew it. I was hoping that leaving this situation cool down the relationship between me and Giulia could have been rebuild more easily; even because what happened wasn't so serious, I thought. Or at least I was hoping so. While I was lost in my reflections about how to manage and fix all this, Tiffany caught me on Facebook chat. I added her a few days before, conveniently arranging my privacy settings so that nobody could see her comments. I was honestly very distracted but nonetheless I started chatting with her, even to check what she had to tell me. I immediately noticed a strong desire from her so that I went to the party with her in a few days. Of course she wasn't saying it openly, but it was easy to understand that she wanted to make sure that I would be there. I told her I would have gone there without letting her understand that I would have stayed with her all the evening: as much as I liked her I'm unsure it would have been the best to spend my whole night with her and have no chance to hook the other girls. Furthermore I still had to see how to cope with the fact the Ilary and Giulia would have been there, not counting that I promised myself to spend a few words with Camilla, because I felt it was the right night. Too much on my dish, I thought. Really too much. How could I cope with all that? The fact that Tiffany and Ilary would be there together wasn't the best, already, not counting that if Giulia had come, I don't know how she could have reacted to the presence of me and Chiara, considering how she kicked us out of her house a few hours earlier. It was a potentially explosive situation and I thought I would have spent the following days thinking about how I could manage it. The main objecting was putting my relationship with Giulia back together or at least, limit the damage waiting and hoping she was ready to forgive me. I knew her well and I also knew that she would have forgiven me. It was only a matter of time and managing the situation at best. I logged out from Facebook and I went for dinner; I was home alone since my parents were out for dinner so I made myself a nice steak. While

I was eating with tv volume at full throttle, I got a message from Ilary. She was asking me about the forthcoming party; she wanted to know if I would have been there. Same as Tiffany, I told her I would have been there without implying that I would have spent my whole night with her. I didn't feel like having my hands tied all night. Neither Ilary nor Tiffany knew about Giulia but I was afraid they would discover it soon. I wasn't the boyfriend of either of them but I felt that they wouldn't have taken it too well knowing that I had a pretty serious relationship with Giulia even if in this period we were not seeing each other very often. Once again I couldn't help noticing how recently difficulties were of a different kind, unlike in the past: the old Luke would have never had three girls in his hands at the same time. Thanks to the improvements of the last weeks my relationships and my results with girls had drastically improved and now the challenges I had to face were different, however suitable for the new myself. I felt somehow stimulated to challenge myself again to see how far I could go: if on one side the old me was suggesting to stay back and not take a risk, my new awareness and the courage that always characterised me were pushing me forward accepting all the difficulties that would have showed up. After all, seen my latest improvement, discovering hidden talents within myself, there wasn't a single reason not to risk. On a t-shirt of a friend of mine I had once read a sentence that said: "Who dares, wins." Nothing truer than that, I thought. As my "friend" Steve Jobs asserted, there was no reason not to follow your own heart. So I decided to set up a proper plan on how to face the various challenges that would outline: the main target was restoring my relationship with Giulia and I felt I could do it. Nevertheless even if I had put my relationship with her back together before friday's party, I wouldn't have known how to cope with the simultaneous presence of Tiffany and Ilary at the sleepover party. A smile came up on my face considering that the old Luke would have never found himself dating so many girls so that he wouldn't even know how to behave. Until now Tiffany and Ilary hadn't met yet or anyway they didn't know that I was dating both of them in the same period. The real problem would have been the party. I decided to relax and I don't know why but I sent a message to Chiara asking her if she had time to meet and talk about how to fix the situation with Giulia. She told me it was ok with her and since the pub was closed she came to my place. A lot time passed since she had come to my house for the very first time and memories impetuously started to surface about the fun we had right a few months before I was with Giulia. I couldn't help noticing how I was partially torn: I didn't feel for Chiara what I felt for Giulia, nevertheless there was attraction and I couldn't hide it. The fact that she was coming to my house awoke a certain excitement in me already, and I felt that if I had really followed my heart, that night, probably we wouldn't have spoken much. But at the same time Giulia was really important to me and I didn't want to hurt her, at least not again. I unplugged my brain for a little while listening to some music, waiting for Chiara: I listened to the song that I had just composed some time before, "Get Down" and that I had already put online on my website: www.LucaGrisendiArt.com I lost myself while listening to this magical song, with my "Beats" earphones on when opening my eyes, lying on the bed I saw Chiara's face. I suddenly got up, understanding that she arrived at the same moment my parents got back from their dinner and she came up with them. "Hi! Did I disturb you?" Chiara asked. "No, no, don't worry. I was only listening to some music." "The song you made? Chiara asked my with a curious look. "Yes, Get Down." I replied "I like it, it's a really nice track." She said nicely. "Thanks!" I replied feeling happy for her appreciation. The best thing was that she ignored that the text was making reference to her. While composing that song, almost unconsciously, I expressed what I really felt for her. What I had inside found a way to express. There was then a moment of silence and of embarrassment, I'd say, in which we both felt that there was a still pretty strong attraction between us that we couldn't deny. If I had to follow my heart I should have jumped on her, throwing her on my bed. "Why can't I do it?" A part of me was wondering and was suffering for the lack of a reply. Chiara broke the silence asking, with a smile on her face that made her look even more irresistible: "What's wrong?" It looked like one of those situations where you date a girl and at some point the attraction gets to such a point that dialogue interrupts, you look at each other for a bit before kissing and then move to the pure physical expression. But in this case my rational self stopped me for respect for the poor Giulia. The usual question bounced on my head: "How can something that gives you pleasure, be so wrong?" With these reflections in my mind and lacking restraint that were about to surrender I trivially replied: "Nothing! Why?" "You look at me as if you wanted to jump on me..." She was brave enough to say. Actually, how can I blame her? The famous feminine sensitivity had grasped the exact feeling that I was experiencing, even if torn between pure passion and cold rationality. I decided to play her game to try to understand if she felt same: "What if it was like that?" I saw her dangerously approaching me with delicate and sexy movements. I realised that even if at a conscious level I was telling myself I couldn't have some fun with Chiara, in this moment the most rational part of my mind was getting the better and the consequences wouldn't have been without pain. In that moment I had no idea how this could end: the thing that astonished me was that also Chiara was pretty eager to get physical despite the previous morning it was her who stopped us for respect of her best friend. She came very close to me and she sat on the bed next to me. She was wearing her killer leggings that in one word were making her irresistible. No man could have resisted her. No one. She started talking in a really sincere way: "I'm really sorry about Giulia... today I couldn't resist and I had to tell her everything because I thought it was the best thing to do. If we had kept it secret too long, she would have taken it even worse and I don't want her to feel worse than this." The attraction of a moment before was suspended while resuming the speech about how to put the situation with Giulia back together and it was replaced by a feeling of mutual understanding about how Giulia could feel now. Nonetheless I felt that Chiara wanted to go way beyond in her speech and she continued: "At the same time I'm torn because I like and I feel something for you. If I hid this from myself maybe you and Giulia could get back together but I couldn't feel good with myself." It was like hearing the words from the last night again, when we met in the pub. The thoughts and the feelings involved were the same. It couldn't be different. We certainly could not turn off the attraction and passion with a simple switch. Then she reached out her hand, softy putting it on mine and asked me: "Do you understand me?" "Of course I do, what you said works for me too. But what about Giulia?" In fact, asking her this, I was implying that I was in and that the only concern was Giulia. Not a small thing, however. We remained silent again, this time physically closer with Chiara's hand now holding mine. Even if on a superficial level we were telling each other we didn't want to do anything, in a deeper level it was clear that the direction we were taking was purely physical. And as I knew, even based on my recent experience with her, it wasn't certainly something that could be stopped in a moment, provided we wanted to stop it. I thought that in life there were moments in which there weren't necessarily only right and wrong choices: in this case if I had made it with Chiara I would have mad myself and her happy but we would have actually hurt Giulia. On the other hand if we hadn't made it, we would have both suffered. So what was the right choice? Probably in certain cases it's only a matter of choice, being ready to accept the consequences. That night, I honestly don't know why, I decided to refrain from doing things I would regret or at least I thought so. Chiara took my hand and put it on her right thigh looking at me right in the eye with a look that didn't allow me to have any doubt. The thighs were not necessarily the part I liked the most in a girl but in that case I felt a momentum of passion that pushed me to letting myself go. After so many words and speech, once more pure passion overwhelmed us. We started kissing very passionately and undressing. Once more, I noticed Chiara's wonderful body which, now naked, appeared in all her beauty. The disquisitions about whether it was right or not to do what we were doing had already gone away. What followed what a powerful and irresistible display of a feeling that had been waiting for too long before it could express itself. Even if we tried to give us reasons not to do it, in the end what we felt right prevailed. It was so pleasant it was breathtaking and we both wanted it to be never ending. While doing it, I realised how uninhibited Chiara was and how she was playing in her field with no fear at all. She was a very cute girl after all and I don't think she had been waiting for me to do it. Here came the surprise! As soon as we finished she confessed that before doing it she was a virgin. I was speechless. She celebrated her birthday in February so she was 18 and I didn't think she was still a virgin. She was a really attractive girl and I thought that in all these months she had gotten it on. It wasn't like that. A part of me was congratulating with myself while the other one was more disapproving. After the moment of pure passion and pleasure, the most rational part of my brain made itself heard and was trying to prevail. I was surprised of how once again Chiara opened up with me proving that what she felt was clearly concrete. She slept with me and the following morning we woke up really late.

Friday, October the 14th

As soon as I opened my eyes and I saw her face next to me on the pillow, I felt a strong sense of happiness. I could clearly smell the scent of her hair wrapping me in a layer of pure pleasure and seeing her hugging me made me feel really touched, feeling her very sweet and vulnerable at the same time. If by only observing her there in my bed I felt a great joy, what had happened couldn't be only a one night stand. And this made things more complicated. She woke up as well and kissed me. We really looked like a couple of fiancée. After all, in that moment, I didn't mind at all. As a matter of fact waking up in the morning with a nice blond girl naked in your bed wasn't that bad. Especially if that blond girl had Chiara's body and face. In such conditions it was impossible to ponder.

Honestly my beloved intuition to which I had given much attention during the last weeks in this precise moment was suggesting me to do it again with Chiara. At least it was more direct and clear than my rational part that often used to get lost in never ending disquisitions. I didn't even have the time to think about it that Chiara was already on me, maybe after feeling what I was feeling. We did it again and it was even better than the previous night. There was even more passion. In a certain way it was even sweeter and more intimate, as if Chiara and I were getting even closer. It was we both wanted, in our deep. I started to understand only in that moment that unlike pure rationality, intuition wasn't something you could control or stop. Once fed it was starting to point out with increasing strength the direction that I had to take; nothing bad just that doing this the relationship with Giulia would have gotten even more complicated. After doing it I stayed in bed with Chiara some more time and in fact I realised that it was like none of us wanted to go away or detach from the other. I felt it very strong. It was almost 11 by then and the sun, up in the sky, coming in from the window was lighting up Chiara's sublime backside, donating as if she was a painting of the 18th century. Her hair was shining of a bright yellow exalted by the sun rays; I wanted to stay there forever.

Maybe pushed by the intimate atmosphere Chiara let herself go with a question that floored me: "Luke, do you believe in love?" "What do you mean?" I replied bewildered. "What do I mean? Do you think that there is someone that you will meet in your life and that you will love from the very first moment and that will be a part of your path forever?" I remained silent for a moment, then I accepted the challenging subject: "I think so... but I also think that to find it, this person, you need to search a lot and for long time and with the risk of suffering a lot. Even if the pain is maybe the way to reach whom you are destined to meet."

I was surprised by my own assertion. I wasn't usually that poetic. "You are right, what you said was really nice." She sweetly replied, putting her head on my chest. "I think that if we listen to our heart and if we are brave enough to do what we have to do, in the end we'll make it to the arms of the person that has always been there for us, ready to love and protect us." I added. Chiara's presence joined with the particular atmosphere was making me especially sensitive or at least it was showing my most sensitive part that used to be hidden. I felt that she really appreciated the word I spent, feeling them hers. We hugged on my bed for another little while. Our bond was strengthening and this was must more incredible thinking that a few days earlier we had only kissed once, with never going further. A part of me was really in need of such a bond with Chiara since the times we kissed before I ended up with Giulia. It was like satisfying a desire and feeding a passion that lied in me from long time, maybe too much. The same was for Chiara and maybe it was even clearer for her.

We both ended in the other's arms because, I suppose, it was right like that.

Despite we tried to slow the things down, what obviously had to happen, happened. The new Luke opened up new scenarios and perspectives that he couldn't even imagine, I thought with a tip of proud. I dared and now I was winning. In my bed with Chiara I felt this taste of victory, this sense of payback against all the frustration that I experienced in the past because I couldn't show I had potential. Now I was finally enjoying the fruits of my work of personal growth and I was aware I still should have changed with perseverance if I wanted to keep this positive trend. And I had no intention to stop. I received a message from Ilary, pretty cheesy, asking me what ever happened to me. I didn't reply right away, as I used to do in the past. "Who was it?" Chiara asked, almost as if she was my girlfriend. "Nobody..." I answered. "I think it was a girl..." She said jokingly. Fortunately she wasn't acting like a girlfriend already.

"Well... might as well, do you think you're the only one in my bed, I mean in my heart?" I answered playing her game. She pretended she got angry and she said: "Probably not, but I'm certainly the one that you desire the most." And here, I must admit, I was floored. She changed from joke to serious in a moment. In that moment I had no idea how to reply such an assertion.

If I had to make a ranking with her, Giulia, Ilary and Tiffany I think Giulia would win even if mine was probably an automatic choice more than really pondered. Actually I really liked Ilary and Tiffany too and for what concerns Chiara...well...having her in my bed was distorting reality. With her naked in front of me asking me this question, the answer seemed to be quite granted. Let's say in that precise moment, it was surely true. And so I told her. "In this precise moment it's like that, you are the one that I desire the most." I said, then kissing her with great passion. I honestly don't know if I was aware that I was creating a bond with Chiara and in a very short time. I thought it was only the new way I took that was leading me to satisfaction and results to me unknown just a month before that day; I was enjoying life in all its shades, including having a beautiful blond girl carving for me, by my side. By then I understood that I would have spent the rest of my day with Chiara and I must say that time seemed to fly; none of us really wanted to split up and I think that in deep we had been waiting for that moment for long time, maybe too much.

We had breakfast and we went shopping together even if I always hated shopping. Who knows why but in that moment it wasn't so bad. Chiara's presence was giving me new energy that was filling me with happiness. The fact that we should have been in school was just a detail. We spoke about all the adventures that we shared in the past like the holiday by the seaside the previous summer and agreed that this moment should have come much earlier.

But clearly we weren't ready and I, in a particular way, wasn't free enough, as I am now. Free to express what I really felt and free to enjoy all the emotions I was experiencing without judging myself. And it was fucking awesome. By dinner time we kissed goodbye with a last, tasty kiss. By now I felt I had completely lost control of the situation. In a rational way, of course. For what concerns emotions, I was feeling rewarded and my instinct had already taken control without letting me the mental disquisitions typical from my past about whether something was right or not. Now I was only acting. Obviously all this was filled with consequences. As soon as I got back home I took a shower, had dinner and then once alone I had the chance to reflect and understand that as marvellous this had been, it surely wouldn't have been easy to manage the relationship with Giulia. I got a message from her in the precise moment saying that she wanted to see me that same night. Nothing else. I accepted right away and she told me the we would have met at her place. I put my iPhone in my pocket, took my Vespa and rushed to her. The same previous day she kicked me out along with Chiara and now she wanted to see me. It was better to permanently abandon logic and let your emotions drive you: life would have been easier, rewarding and full of glitches. I thought that this could be considered a great lesson learnt thanks to the Test. I would have shared it with the old John.

CHAPTER 16

OPENING GIVES YOU THE
KEY TO FORGIVENESS

Friday, October the 14th

That night the party of one of the girl from the school had been postponed due to reasons I didn't know. Once in front Giulia's house, I gave her a flash and she immediately opened. As soon as I saw her, I immediately understood why she had always been the very number one for me. That evening she had something particular that was making her so beautiful and so sweet at the same time. In that moment I felt like shit for what I had done with Chiara; I always considered myself a good guy and I didn't like to lie. I didn't always tell her the truth but I wasn't cheating on her and not with her best friends and then hiding the whole thing. In that moment I told myself I should have told her but I was overwhelmed from her physical appealing; she jumped on me and we did it on the kitchen table with incredible intensity and passion. I didn't even the chance to speak before doing it. Obviously I really liked that but how come after screaming after me the day before now she was jumping on me? Then I thought about my willing to definitely abandon logic views. I had to talk about it with John the day after because I was sure we would have came up with interesting considerations. Half of me was shocked, I mean in a positive sense: going to bed twice with Chiara and now with Giulia, one after the other, was simply great. My self esteem got higher and higher. I could feel that while doing it Giulia was more sweet while Chiara was wilder. I appreciated both styles. Giulia interrupted my usual thoughts:

"You know Luke, I thought about the relation between you and Chiara and I think although you were with my best friends, after all in this period we weren't seen each other so a part of me would like to forgive you. But the other part hates you to death for what you did. I am fighting with myself and I don't now if I can still trust you and I don't know if I can really forgive you completely." I could feel clearly the conflict inside her and I avoided to express my usual mental considerations knowing that they couldn't take me anywhere and at that point I decided to confess. I don't know why I did that. I had this beautiful girl naked beside me and I could feel that she wanted to forgive me and in a way she already did it: I didn't want to lie to her or hiding anything anymore. Even if lately I had great results with girls and this changed me, my sincere and pure part was still alive in me and was refusing to fool Giulia around. What I said was simply: "I slept with Chiara…" These exact words came out from my mouth, like if I could not stop them. I was prepared to the worst. After a moment of silence, peace before the storm: "What?" She asked surprised. "You fucked Chiara?" She added trying to be more clear. I answered a feeble "Yes…" She stood up and ran away crying and screaming: "How could you?" "Shit" I thought. "What have I done?" I was there lying like a fool for a few seconds and then I stood up and went to the room where she locked herself. I was lucky, their parents weren't there. "Giuly, I am sorry!" I screamed in front of her door while she was clearly crying. I did a damn stupid thing. Yes, but the stupid thing was sleeping with Chiara or telling Giulia about it? "Giuly, please open the door, I am so sorry…really!" She opened the door just to scream at me with her face covered by tears: "How could you sleep with her? I had already forgiven you!" She shut the door on my face again. Honestly I didn't now how to react. In the past I wouldn't have had the chance to sleep with Chiara so I couldn't hurt Giulia. But at the same time I would have never lived those moments of pure strong passion with Chiara. My diplomatic side had to admit that making everybody happy was impossible. It was clear that intuition guided you on the path "right" for you without caring about someone else's feelings. I don't know. Even if the truth was hurting, I was feeling better after I told her no matter what it would have happened. I was feeling better with myself even if at the same time I understood how much I made her suffer. I promised myself that I would have done anything to deserve her forgiveness and to get her back.

Finally I could get inside her room and I sat down on her bed next to her. She was crying and she was sad as never before. I was really feeling as a shit for the way I made her feel. She was still naked and lying on the bed: I thought that a girl that beautiful and intelligent didn't deserve to feel that way. It was my job now to psych her up. I tried out a physical contact to made her feel how sorry I was. I started talking to her sweetly: "I can imagine how you feel in this moment and believe me, I feel so bad for what I have done. I know there are no excuses for what happened and I decided to tell you everything because even if you are suffering now, I think it would have been worse If you never knew the truth. I couldn't hide myself. You know how I am. For good and for bad, I have always been a good guy." In my relating with Giulia I have always been faithful in the past and cheating on her with Chiara was the only unfaithful episode. In my defense I knew that in these weeks Giulia and I weren't seen each other and anyway I immediately told Giulia about my little crash on Chiara. I probably didn't acted that bad, at least I hoped so. She stopped crying and she hugged me very strong looking for some support. She said: "I am confused, I wanted to forgive you for the kiss and now you're telling me that you slept with her..." She was sobbing and hugging me so I felt I had to comfort her and I answered: "I know, honey. I am so sorry. I told you the truth cause I could never lie to you. You know I could never hide something like this. I have always been faithful in the past and this thing happened with Chiara in these days and..." She interrupted me: "And what? We take a little break and you sleep with my best friend?" I promptly answered: "To be fair you left me, we didn't decide to take a break. And I think that Chiara has her own responsibilities too." After a moment of silence, Giulia asked me: "Do you remember the very first time we met? I was surprised from that question and I couldn't stop myself from thinking about that magic moment. Giulia and I met each other during a pool party few months before in July. I remember that Chiara was at the party too and I clearly remembered the images of me and Chiara kissing each other at night on the pool. That day I noticed Giulia for her beauty and her sweetness and after I had the chance to know her better. But then I had been overwhelmed by Chiara's passion and helped by a few drinks, I ended up kissing her. Anyhow, after a few days, I added Giulia on my facebook contact in order to ask her if she wanted to go out with me. I kept seeing Chiara for a few weeks more but I considered that a summer crash while with Giulia I started dating seriously from the beginning of september and from that moment I stopped seeing Chiara. I had this flashback before answering her: "Oh right, the party on the pool. You had that bathing suite that made you look fabulous. And I immediately noticed you. I remember you spit a cocktail on me too." I said smiling, hoping to relieve the tension. I felt she was feeling better than before and then she said: "I noticed you because you were smart, funny and you seemed different from the others. Different from the other guys who use girls just to sleep with them and then cheat on others girls leaving them alone..." I understood what she meant. I behaved exactly like the all the other guys she was talking about, and I deceived trust she had in me. Anyway, it was true that I didn't use her nor abandoned her. I just made a mistake and that was the reason I was there, to try to get over it. I felt she secretly understood this, without telling me. We laid holding each other and we fell asleep in her bed. She didn't put her pigiama back on: it was so intimate and special, just sleeping with her, naked in that bed, I wished that could be the beginning of a new real relationship.

Saturday, October the 15th

I woke up the next morning and this time, instead of Chiara, GIulia was hugging me in the bed. Her skin was soft and her curvy and sexy body was making my awakening very special. My feelings for Giulia was something different from what I felt in the morning for Chiara. It was something more deep and strong. She woke up too and we started kissing in a very romantic way. After a while she said: "You know Luke, I think that after all that happened, I can forgive you. There aren't guys like you around and I don't want to lose you..." I felt extremely gratified and very happy by her words. Then she added: "Nevertheless, the only way to know if you care enough for me is letting the weekend pass and see what happens. There is a pajama party next Friday night and many hot chicks are going to be there. You're free to do what you feel. This is the only way for you to know if you care enough for me or not..." I was very surprised by her words and I didn't know what to say. The fact that she was already forgiving me shocked me and now she was telling me I could feel free for the weekend.

This definitely was a Test! She was showing a good self confidence leaving me the chance to act the way I wanted on a pajama party. I was admiring her, this was quite special. I thought I could have some fun with Ilary and Tiffany and then think about dating seriously Giulia again. Theoretically I already knew I was going to get back with Giulia but with everything that happened lately, with all the new chances I had with girl, well, nothing was definite. I made her understand I agreed. We were on a school holiday that day so we didn't have to hurry to school. Caught in a passion impetus, I hugged her making her feel what I wanted. We made love with great intensity. This was the best answer to my questions. I've alway been fascinated by the way physical language was much more expressive and effective to me in linking people and help them communicate. This was the best way nature gave us to share a feeling, becoming a whole with one another, one entity. In that moment, without even saying a word, I was feeling connected to that beautiful girl in a deep and magic way. I enjoyed that moment in all its fullness: I enjoyed Giulia's curves with my hands feeling her full breast with my fingers. No other sensation could be more pleasant. We laid there for a while, trying to extend that moment which was making up us with each other. Giulia had always been a special girl to me, different from the others and I couldn't describe the way I felt when she was next to me. Nevertheless, there was something, a force coming from my latest improvements that was pushing me beyond towards new paths, towards new girls. I was pushed by the confidence I had assimilated lately; if I was able to express and show my potential getting the best results out of it, how could I limit myself to a monogamous relation with Giulia? I thought I could feel prisoner and that, once back together, I would leave her. Or what if I had got back together with her, without being satisfied of my relation: I would have cheated on her. I didn't want to do that. Giulia's phone rang, I give it to her and I saw it was Chiara calling. Giulia answered and moved to another room. I kept thinking but I could partly hear the conversation. I heard Chiara admitting what her best friend already knew. This time I was the one that anticipated the whole thing to her. I was expecting some quarrels but, luckily, I could hear and feel their friendship was stronger than anything else. Giulia herself had always been a good girl who couldn't feel resentment and she forgave us quite easily.

I have to admit that I appreciated her attitude very much and my esteem towards her grew even more: after all it wasn't simple to accept what Chiara and I did. This was the reason why I knew I had to treat her right not making her suffer in the future. I really had to be sure before getting back with her.

I knew I had to think about the whole thing very carefully, and I decided to make my decision after the week end. I listened to what they were saying and it seemed that Giulia was accepting excuses from her best friend. They had always been good friends, they shared may different experiences and their friendship grew trough years. What happened in the last days someway represented an indelible mark in their friendship but I wanted their relation to survive and continue. I was guilty as Chiara was and I didn't want for Giulia to lose her friend and viceversa. The call ended and Giulia came back in the room, laying next to me. She hugged me smoothly touching me with her breast. She was still naked, so was I, and I could see her beautiful perfect body standing there in all its beauty. After a short moment of silence, I asked her what happened during the telephone call with Chiara. "Everything ok, I think. She said she is very sorry, that she didn't mean to hurt me and that she loves me very much. She also said what happened with you was just a weak moment...." She said with a smooth voice. Then she added: "I feel I can forgive her...." I immediately answered: "I understand, well I think so. I hope you can forgive us both. We surrender to temptation and we have no excuses for this."

She didn't say anything else and she hugged again, stronger than before. I could feel our heart near to each other more than ever. She told me Chiara was coming by later that afternoon to talk about the whole situation so she kindly asked me if I could leave. "No problem" I answered. I really wanted to get over this. I wanted to solve the situation in the best way. I told her I wanted to sty with her till Chiara's arrival. She was happy and we laid in the bed until the early afternoon. I took breakfast in bed for her trying to be romantic and make her understand that, despite what happened, she was so special to me. We talked about our relationship and all the nice experiences we shared till that moment; we weren't dating from a long time but we had a lot of fun together. We built a strong and beautiful relationship and I didn't want everything to end because of what happened with Chiara. I could feel things were turning fine: Giulia on one side, who was a very mature girl strong enough to forgive us; Chiara and I, on the other side, doing our best to deserve it. Exactly like we did with Chiara, we could go back with our mind to the party during which we met. Giulia underlined that during that party I ended going with Chiara before her. This detail made her curious. "I remember you looking at me that night but at the end when I saw you kissing with Chiara, I felt hopeless." I interrupted her: "Oh, you saw me kissing Chiara? I thought you were inside, with that guy..." "Who, the guy with glasses? Absolutely not. He probably dreamt of it but nothing happened. I like you..." She looked at me straight in the eyes and she kissed me sweetly.

Then she said: "You liked Chiara more than me and maybe it's still that way. What does she have more?" I couldn't get if she had said so as a provocation or if she really had meant it. Anyway I tried to reassure her and tell her what I felt. "You're two girls, someway similar to each other, and very different in an other way. At the party last year I was a little high so I can't consider that moment. If I am here now is because you're the only person in my heart. You are the special one who has something that Chiara will never have..."

I was talking with my heart and I was honest. For the second time in two days I was opening myself and I started understanding that this was the key to my important improvement. Anyway I knew that with this new attitude I was risking to be hurt more easily. In the end I felt this was the path I had to go trough.

The day before I told Chiara that she was the girl I wanted the most in this moment and now I just told Giulia she was the only one in my heart. I think I was honest in both cases. I said what I was feeling in that particular moment without any deep speculation if it was logic or not wanting a girl and knowing, at the same time, that another one was the right one for you. I started thinking how things would have turned with Chiara. What would have I felt if a saw her? And what would have she done knowing that we wouldn't see each other anymore? I would have had my answers very soon. So Giulia answered: "Are you serious?" I answered promptly: "Sure, I really feel this for you. I'm sorry if what happened made you think something different." She didn't answer but she hugged me strong again. I could feel our relation was mending after the terrible moment of the day before and I started thinking she would have been the only one for the next months. I left her around lunch time because Chiara was on her way. For one moment I thought about us three, naked on the bed, having crazy fun. This gave me a nice feeling and a little voice in my head started telling me everything could have happened. I listened to the voice without judging and I thought nothing was impossible, thinking back to everything that happened in these last two weeks. I kissed Giulia goodbye and ran down the stairs with the taste of her mouth still in mine. I went home for lunch. There was a school strike that day so we were off: good, I needed to think....

CHAPTER 17

THE DILEMMA

In the first part of the afternoon I chatted with John on Facebook sharing the latest happenings and in particular my considerations. He said that he was experimenting the same things with a girl he was dating. It seemed as if by growing together we were living the same happenings and living the same feelings that were taking us towards higher levels of awareness. We were sharing the success and this was making the path I was following even more pleasant and satisfactory. We agreed on the fact that at this point what made a difference was a more opening to witness the stronger self esteem reached by now. In the past we wouldn't have reached this awareness first of all because we wouldn't have had the chance to make all these experiences and we wouldn't have this self esteem, now acquired, that allowed us to be more open but also more vulnerable. The price to pay to be more open was a higher risk to be hurt, but without any doubt, it was worth while. While talking, we decided to change the rules of the Test so that the guys now could get up to under the sheets with the girls, so capitalizing the great job accomplished up to now.

We thought this was the right thing to do, the more natural step forward that allowed all the guys to give a value to the growing reached in these weeks.

We realized how this spirit of personal improvement was familiar to all of us not only to myself and John. In these weeks a lot of guys had put themselves at stake and had experienced new things. Behaviors, ways of acting, approaches and mental attitudes that in the past they had never practiced, were now helping everyone to obtain fantastic results. If by changing the rules the Test was considered technically finished was not important to us since the project was just a way and not the aim. A way to help us which was giving fantastic results to all the guys of our high school. This was important, nothing else.

Once the decision was taken and after Jack's, Robert's and Simon's approval who was online in that moment, we informed all the guys of the school on Facebook about the change just introduced. In a matter of a few minutes a lot of "like" arrived and by reading the comments we understood that we had made the right choice. Considering the imminence of Friday night's party, it made even more sense. It was as if the party could be used to all of us as a final test about everything learnt up to now, and by understanding this we were all very excited to "start the job". While I was on line chatting, I was caught by Tiffany who had changed her profile picture with another one taken at the seaside last summer with some of her friends. This was a "dangerous" picture, I thought. I had just left Giulia and temptations were many. The higher abilities acquired and disclosed during the last weeks were bringing higher possibilities and therefore things were not necessarily easier. Without doubts I was happier now than in the past but sometimes I was also undecided about the right choice to make. Giulia was extremely important to me, I had no doubts about this, but how could this be enough considering my potentialities? This was not a rhetorical question. More than likely the answer would have been the reason for my next step in my personal growth path. Apparently there was no univocal answer or better there was no answer at all. After all by following my instinct as I was doing now, I had got up to where logics had not a say in the matter and this meant very often not to consider the consequences. This was extremely dangerous though, when at stake there were the feelings of other girls and even if now I was able to do things I would have never thought of in the past, I still considered myself a guy that respected others' feelings. At this point I thought that perhaps my 'being respectful' may have due to my past limits. In other words, I was convincing me that I didn't want to hurt some girls by cheating them but actually in many cases I wouldn't have been able to do it, even desiring so. Surely there was still a part of me that respected what girls were feeling but probably there was not anymore the other part that justified the 'not going with other girls' as a form of respect. I was telling me that I didn't want to cheat a girl for a form of respect when actually a part of the motivation, not all of it, was due to my incapacity to do it. Now instead, since I had no limits and part of this justification was missing, the doubt about my behavior was concrete. Moreover I didn't want to hurt Giulia and this was without a doubt.

I chatted with Tiffany for a while and I understood that she was willing to see me as soon as possible: I also saw Ilary on line and it came to my mind the message she had sent me and my ignoring it. I had just picked up my iPhone when she caught me chatting, therefore I found myself chatting with these two chicks wondering how to avoid screwing up. They both were insisting, even if it wasn't done openly, to meet before Friday night's party. I think they wanted to meet in a private and more cozy place so I understood what their aim was.

At this point though, I did not break the rules anymore therefore I was a little bit calmer, besides it was true that it was Giulia herself that said, in a moment of courage or maybe madness, I could be 'free' for the weekend. It meant to enjoy myself with Tiffany and Ilary without feeling guilty at all. And surely I didn't mind this. Therefore I was in the mood to work on it without thinking too much. First I kept them both on thorns for a while just to have fun and see to what point I could get. After all the spirit of the Test was still vivid in me which was pushing me to experiment and dare like I had never done before. The party was very close, just a few days ahead, so I decided to accept both Tiffany's and Ilary's invitation to meet them before the pajama party. Some afternoons with them would have been a great occasion to enjoy this period and to understand if it was a matter of quick affairs or more serious relations. I was thinking and meditating as usual about the next steps to take when I was interrupted by a sms from Chiara that stated she had talked to Giulia. She asked to meet me that same night in order to talk about it. I thought it was rather dangerous to see Chiara at night considering what had happened in the last period. I agreed saying to prefer seeing her before dinner, in order to water down a possible desire that could take us to a situation to feel sorry for later on. She accepted and said she would arrive at seven o'clock. I kept chatting to Ilary and Tiffany for the rest of the afternoon and I must admit that I enjoyed even just joking and provoking her. It was just an anticipation of the fact that we would have met in the next days and this was charging me up a lot. Besides having Giulia's 'approval' everything was easier. Now I was really curious to see how things would have evolved with Chiara when we had to meet before dinner. Would there have been an escalation of pure passion that had overwhelmed us some days ago? Or our more rational side would have prevailed? Maybe it was just a flame died down by now. In a few hours I would have known it. I told Tiffany and Ilary we could agree to meet the following Monday at school; I know I took the high risk to be seen by the other one, but besides liking the risk I was so sure of myself that I simply didn't consider it a problem at all. In that very moment I felt to act in that way so without too many doubts I did it. Then I went to take a shower and in half an hour Chiara arrived at my house and rang the bell. I opened the door and welcomed her in my attic where I had my bedroom. I couldn't avoid noticing that I liked her tremendously and I couldn't hide to myself that a part of me was attracted by her in a very strong way. I feared that we could have let ourselves go and even if it would have been incredibly pleasant and liberative, it would have caused big suffering to Giulia. "Hi, how did it go?" I asked Chiara. "Fine….I guess so. I've seen her deeply hurt for what has happened and honestly I've felt disgust for having made her feel that way. I have tried all ways to convince her that I felt displeased and also the fact of having called her to admit what I had done, even if she already knew it from you, shows the heavy sense of guilt that I felt. I hope she understood how bad I feel. I don't want our beautiful friendship to be ruined by what happened." She spoke with her voice full of emotion. I knew how strong their friendship was and how important each one was in the other one's life. She kept on saying: "Giulia is too important for me, too much…" She lowered her eyes and I could feel clearly how sad she was for what she had done. I wondered if we would have talked about us too and the answer arrived right away. "I don't think that anything changed from the first night I talked to you in the pub. I still have feelings for you and my sense of guilt can't abandon me…" She added. Her sadness had changed into a sense of guilt. She liked me and after what we had done, betraying Giulia's trust, things were not that simple now. She added: "I know I can't and never will be able to stay with you and I guess I must convince myself of it…" Surely, like Chiara said, going to bed together in the last days had not certainly simplified things. We had done what we felt like but unluckily it couldn't work. I answered:

"I understand what you mean. I went to Giulia's myself, I apologized and at this point I don't want to do anything that can hurt her. Even if you are terribly attractive to me." I added this openly. It was true and I couldn't and didn't want to hide it to me nor to her. I saw her face lighting up suddenly as if my words had allowed for a moment to forget her inside conflict and to feel appreciated. "Do you really find me attractive?" She asked with a sweet voice. "Of course. Giulia has a special place in my heart but at the same time I feel incredibly attracted by you..." I realized that in the last days my words had made both Chiara and Giulia feel very special and all this was making everything even more confusing. Anyway it was what I was actually feeling and it was not to just make them feel better. I myself, like Chiara didn't know how to behave now. The dilemmas remained the same and even if I had spoken to Giulia my feelings were contrasting. Giulia was very special to me but at the same time I couldn't deny that Chiara was able to cause strong attraction on me. My dear instinct showed in a very clear way the way to take but I decided to make an exception to the rule and decided not to listen to it notwithstanding in the last weeks I had decided to be less rational and more instinctive. Chiara interrupted my thoughts: "I am sad, you know. At this point I don't feel like behaving like we did the last time. Even if it has been so pleasant..." She said it biting her lip. I honestly started feeling all excited. Even if she had said to be sad, I felt she was excited more than sad. What we felt for each other was evident and once again, even if we talked in a certain way, a thin but powerful force was slowly bringing us close physically. I got closer, I put my hand on her face to move her hair and said with a sweet and soft tone of voice: "I know what you are feeling and believe me I'd wish we were free to express our emotions openly. But we cannot. I've just seen Giulia and I can't cheat her again, I really cannot. Moreover we well know that it would be an uphill path..." Chiara turned slightly her waist and hugged me looking straight at me. Her dark eyes were watching me restless and I could feel that passion was growing out of control. I could smell her fantastic perfume and her long blond hair was simply irresistible. In that moment I really couldn't understand, as I had already noticed, how something so pleasant could be wrong. Anyway just thinking of Giulia crying because of me and Chiara made me stop and understand that nothing could happen that night. Chiara herself, I realized, didn't want to go further. We remained still in a hug but understanding that the right thing was stopping there. Useless to admit that a part of us would have liked to enjoy the moment but our rational side prevailed at the end. In spite of that we didn't know how to handle the issue. Even avoiding pleasant involvement in future, we would have met at school anyway and sometimes with Giulia as well and the desire would have remained strong the same. Perhaps it would have even increased due to our forced distance. To eliminate the sincere feeling that each of us was feeling wasn't the positive thing to do: surely we could avoid hurting Giulia which was the main purpose, but what at what price for our feelings? I felt I could be happy with Giulia and the challenges in front of me would have let me understand if she was the right person for me. I knew deep inside that a few days wouldn't have magically settled things and on Monday morning I wouldn't have felt too different from now. Tiffany and Ilary were just affairs, this is what I thought, while Chiara was something more. Moreover I had promised to myself to get to know Camilla since my instinct was telling me that something interesting could start with her. I thought that maybe the results obtained up to now were above my capacity of handling them: at this point I was seeing too many girls without any clear idea in my mind. Anyway it was difficult to think that my growth up to now couldn't grant the necessary instruments to handle the situation: more than likely I still had to understand a lot of things. Instinct was not enough. It could show you the right way but I suppose that your capacity of learning and reasoning was just as important. If not, I would have found myself in bed with Giulia one day, with Chiara another day and then with Ilary and Tiffany too. From a certain point of view that thought was like heaven, in particular for the old Luke's standards, but on the other hand it was like hell since I felt that I wouldn't have had any real satisfying relation with any of the girls, besides having to lie and hurt Giulia. To cut it short, senseless results without criterion and possibility to have a long period relation. Just a total chaos full of sex. I lingered with Chiara for a while and since my parents were out for dinner I invited her to stay. I wanted to believe that without making sex I could prolong my time with her. But this would not solve anything. I prepared her dinner and I think I showed my most romantic side, a double edged weapon that could have caused more attraction. I chose the moment to express her my surprise of knowing that she was still a virgin when we had sex together the first time. She answered immediately feeling provoked by my statement: "You are surprised because you may have always thought that I was the common blond chick that loves having fun and sex with all the guys. When we had petting at the swimming pool party last summer I had drunk too much but I was bright enough to know that I kissed you because I really liked you, not just for the sake of a party." "I understand." I answered leaving her the chance to go on because I was curious to hear what she could say. "We've dated each other before you started a relation with Giulia but we've never got up to sex and once you started with her my hopes weakened. I hoped you could be the first one for me, that's why I've never really looked for any summer affairs." "In other terms, it's just as if you had waited for me." I said sure to have understood. "Well, in a certain way it's lake that." She spoke pointing her big eyes on mine. "At the end you've obtained what you desired, waiting has paid you back." I added. "Yes and I must say it was worthy waiting." She said making me feel really great. "Unluckily I'm afraid there won't be a following..." She added lowering her eyes. I was feeling between two forces pulling me in two different directions: on one side there was Chiara for which my attraction was increasing more and more after knowing she had waited for me to lose her virginity and on the other side there was Giulia that I had always considered my ideal girlfriend. As I had already considered, in this case I didn't think there was a real right thing to do, there was simply a choice to make being ready to accept the responsibilities of the consequences. That was all. Chiara gave me her compliments for the nice dinner I had prepared and I felt that a story between us could work. Unluckily, even if at the moment I was free to express what I was feeling enjoying new and fantastic experiences, I knew I could not just have fun with her anymore. And a part of me was saying it wasn't right: on the contrary I should have given total freedom to my feelings since that was the only way to enjoy my life upmost. I was young and full of potential that I had showed only partially in the last weeks. My truest and deepest part was encouraging me to follow my heart without control and restraint. I knew Chiara felt the same. In some ways I knew that sometimes our hearts were beating in unison; we were in perfect harmony and not having sex together while deeply feeling like it would have been against our most sincere desire. And would have made us tremendously unhappy. Once we finished eating, we both were feeling this latent, unexpressed energy waiting for our courage to get us closer and become just one thing: in this case, different from the other times, it seemed that our mind prevailed on our heart. And the passion that had attracted each other risked to be withdrawn in a shell without any chance to come out. Even after dinner, Chiara stayed at my house. None of us wanted to separate even if it was not said openly; it was evident how strong was the chemistry for each other. It was a feeling far beyond the words, beyond the pure rationality and beyond what we thought was the right thing: it was simply a strong and sincere emotion that was ready to be lived to the most, in a whirlpool of pleasure that would have overwhelmed us totally. It was impossible not to think of this and it was not enough to move our attention and look somewhere else. As I had the chance to find out in the last weeks, the passionate and restless irrationality handled by instinct and fed by the heart could not be controlled or limited and finished to prevail all the time. It did not care of the consequences, positive or negative. It was simply working. It showed. And it allowed to reach the top of pleasure, so high not to think it was possible. In that very moment what I knew in my heart to be done was to make love to Chiara so deeply and intensely to make her screams of pleasure be heard all over the neighborhood. I have always considered sex as the main and most powerful way to communicate between a guy and a girl. It was the way that allowed you to be linked to a girl to such a deep level that no verbal language could ever equal or express. When you make love to a girl in such a passionate and emotional way, it is possible to go beyond one's limited and mortal nature and reach a completely different dimension, much higher and made of pure pleasure. I think the Hinduism considers sex a way to transcend one's mortal reality. I totally agree. Just what I thought. Chiara and Giulia could make me feel emotions that would enrich my life in a way that I never would have imagined. I couldn't but realize that only when you overpass your fears you start to really live. Living with fear or limited by fear is not actually living.

It is a way to survive, mere existence without any significance. Only having the courage to follow one's heart, whatever it can tell us, we become free, fundamental condition of the human being. We were generated to explore and conquer, run, fall and get up again. The only thing not to be done is remain idle, closed up in our fears. In this way a part of us, the more superficial one, will make us believe that we are "happy" and that nothing must be changed. Slowly though, we'll let die the flame that burns bountiful in the deepest of our soul, that vital sparkle that makes us unique and can lead us to unexpected horizons. It takes guts to listen and feed and follow this lymph that runs inside of us, it is probably the most difficult thing but also the only thing that can make us really "Happy". Courage is always rewarding. Only the few that give value to this courage, following one's dreams every single day, can really love life in all its shades and feel "Alive". This powerful observation resonated in me. I sat on the couch with Chiara and started watching a movie, may be the wrong one. It was the story of a high school guy torn between two girls; the likeness was tremendous. We found us clasped in a sweet hug, almost as a close couple. In some ways we felt very good together. I said freely: "Chiara what can we do?"

She turned her head, showed me her beautiful face and she kissed me on my lips tenderly. Then she said: "We cannot hide our feelings. When we made love the other day it has been wonderful and I will never forget it. I wish we did it again many, many times...." I felt my heart beat faster and faster and without realizing it I started hugging Chiara close to me. Her perfume and taste were incredibly exciting and were inexorably demolishing my inhibitions. The transgression of the situation was making it even more attractive. Anyway I felt that none of us wanted to make the first move because each of us hoped it was the other one to either start or stop it. In any case the hesitation was hanging over us. None of us was ready to let ourselves go. I said to her: "I've just apologized with Giulia so if we had sex now, I think I would be destroyed by the sense of guilt. Unluckily I think that the right thing to do is...not to do anything." Chiara was very understanding: "I know, you are right. I think it's better to leave this behind. This is right towards Giulia...." We agreed about this but it was evident that our hearts were feeling totally different. If we had not allowed the desire so strong inside of us to express, we would have never reached the so longed happiness. A part of us, I guess the most important one, wouldn't have obtained what so greatly desired and the consequences of it would have been heavy to bear. In that moment the right thing would have been to make love intensely and no stop. The right thing according to which principle? Giulia would never understand and also a part of me would not agree on making sex to Chiara. It was just a question of seeing which part would have prevailed. I had given up to the evidence that 'right' or 'wrong' were very relative concepts. In that moment I did my best to avoid what had happened the night before. One thing was having fun with Tiffany and Ilary in the weekend and even Giulia had given me her permission, but it was another thing to make love again to her best friend. Moreover, we had apologized to her. We really could not do it. We lingered tightly hugged without going further keeping our strong desire under control. We talked all night, joking and having a great time anyway. It was not the same but I found Chiara's company very pleasant anyway as a simple friend even if I wanted so much more. Before the night was over, to my great surprise, she asked to stay overnight. For a moment I could not answer then I agreed. It was incredible but we both did not want to renounce each other's company and we couldn't fully express this strong desire though so the only thing to do was prolonging our time together. She spent the night over and obviously it was pleasant and exciting at the same time. She didn't have any pajamas with her so I offered my shorts but she preferred to sleep just in her panties and one of my T-shirts. As soon as she took off her jeans I was shocked and breathless at the sight of her butt as perfect as a sculpture. She didn't miss that and smiled at me. It was clear that she was provoking me but not in a cocky and shameless way. She had forced herself not to have sex but a part of her wanted it badly. And she was trying her best to get up to the no return point. When seeing her strong thighs I felt like it was time to jump on her. But I thought about Giulia's face, her big blue eyes, so I stopped. I could not do this to her. We went under the sheets to sleep but even if it was late and the light was off none of us could go to sleep. We kept talking expressing our desire only with words, never going further. For what we were saying and the way we were talking, it was clear that passion was very heavy in the air. Attraction was very strong and now that Chiara was wearing just her little underwear, without her brow, I was about to let myself go. Plus her smell was more good than ever. We joked the whole time and I noticed that little by little she was approaching me physically until she asked me: "How was your first time?" She was lying towards me on one side, with her beautiful blond hair on the pillow. I smiled quietly. She was picking on me and I liked it. This was exciting me too. "Why this indiscreet question?" I asked."Oh, is it a secret? You already know about my first time..." She said winking at me. I thought about love we made few days before and how much I liked it "Yeah, actually..." I only answered. She started caressing my hair. "Was it as good as with me?" My last defenses started to fall apart and the non turning point was there. I answered sincerely: "It was so nice with you that I would like to.." and I stopped. "Do it again...now?" she asked. I sigh covering my indecision. I continued: "Chiara, you know how things are. I'm incredibly attracted from you and I would love to make love with you....now all night long. You are an incredible passionate girl and I'm sure we could have fun but I just apologized to Giulia and I can still see her cute face with her big blue eyes looking at me..." I said sincerely. I would have loved to let myself go with her. In the past I would have paid for an occasion like that but I couldn't do anything in this moment. She immediately answered: "I understand you and I feel the same". I did apologies with Giulia as well and I don't want to hurt her again. I mean it. But I feel this incredibly strong desire for you pushing me towards you and I can't ignore it." Then she added:" How can something so nice be wrong?". I was surprised she had my same doubts. It seemed Chiara and I were connected in a such a deep and intimate level that made us share the same thoughts. I was astonished. The same question I asked myself was now coming from outside waiting for an answer. Probably the problem was not the answer but acting knowing already what to do. It was happening often that I was telling myself I didn't know what to do in a confused situation, when I actually knew it perfectly; but I did not act consequently. Because the change was hard and conscious or not I always knew what to do to improve. The problem was doing it. So the problem was doing what I already knew. I felt she was sincere even if the contradiction was clear. She wanted to respect her best friend but at the same time attraction was very strong. I started thinking about girls and how they are driven by emotions and pure unreason a lot more than us guys. I could have judged her, noticing she was about to betray her best friend's trust after apologizing but I would have made a wrong evaluation: girls were thinking in a complete different way from us guys. Logic, in this case, was useless and passion would have won at the end, right or wrong. I knew how good we could feel if we just let ourselves go, expressing ourselves but my deepest and rational part was stooping me. For the first time I felt like even my emotional part was keeping me because If I thought about Giulia, I was feeling many strong emotions. So it wasn't just my rational part talking to me but even the irrational part was responsible for my behavior. Finally I understood that for the biggest part of my life I was driven by emotions, feelings and love. This thought could represent another little step in my personal growth path started a few weeks before; plus I realized how these considerations came in particular moments. In other words, every time I stepped out from my comfort zone and I pushed myself beyond what I thought were my limits: it was obvious that the only way to grow was facing with bravery all the situations doing what I thought I had to do. Now, the voice guiding me was stronger than in the past or maybe I could hear it better. I was thinking about all this before answering Chiara "I undestand you, my little Chiaras...I know how you feel, because I feel the same. You know, dear, in these last weeks I did my best to follow my instinct without thinking too much and in this case, I know that I would like and I should make love to you. But a part of me could never cheat on Giulia anymore and I prefer not to". I felt her disappointment but immediately after I could feel her respect for me. I was doing something difficult to respect Giulia. Anyway, Chiara herself wasn't sure. My deny was helping her making her own decision or maybe she just didn't have any other chance. After a moment of silence which seemed timeless she said: "I respect you choice and I admire you. Most of the guys, probably all of them, wouldn't have cared for their girlfriends. You, with me in the same bed, are stopping yourself for respect to Giulia. She is lucky she has you and I think she knows it." Then she kissed my gently on my lips helping me understand, together with her words, that I *did the right thing*. We stopped talking and we slowly fell asleep. She hugged me and we slept like that all night long.

CHAPTER 18

CARPE DIEM

Sunday, October the 16th

We spent all Sunday together and once again I had chance to observe how I was changing. In the past I would have never gained such a great pleasure from simply talking to a beautiful girl. I really was another Luke! I was proud. Chiara stayed at my place all day and even in the evening she gave no sign of leaving me. She stayed the night once again to sleep (just that). I was really enjoying all this even if it was only strengthening our relationship making the situation with Giulia even more complicated. After an intense day, Chiara hugged me very sweetly and we slept together. I was seriously beginning not to be able to stay without her.

Monday, October the 17th

I woke up in the morning and I saw Chiara's beautiful face towards me. She was already awake and she was looking at me, with a soft smile that was standing out for her delicate features. "Good morning!" She said with a cheerful tone. "Errrr...good morning." I muttered, still half asleep. "Slept well?" Chiara asked me, already wide awake. "Yeah, great. Did you hug me all night?" I asked her. "Yes and I liked it, a lot." She replied, making me already feel well early in the morning. I brought her the breakfast in bed because I enjoyed making her feel good and even if couldn't make love, at least I had the chance to show her that I cared. She really appreciated it and I noticed how such little things always made an impression on girls. We dressed up, she hopped on my Vespa and we went to school. Arrived there she got off, took off her helmet and she started heading to her class without saying anything and without waiting for me. "Hey, what are you doing? Not waiting for me?" I asked her, but she didn't reply and kept walking. Then I added: "Chiara, is everything alright?" She turned around with a sad look and told me: "No, it's not alright. If I can't be with you, I will never be truly happy." So she kept walking and I let her go. I really understood how she felt or at least I thought I knew. In that precise moment, once again, I realised how things had changed for me. My problems weren't having a girl to date on Saturday night but being able to manage several relationships all together. Really incredible if not all this was normal to me. I got into the classroom and met the old John. He confirmed that the change we made to the rules that we arranged that actually ended the Test, was the right thing. Speaking of the Test, he told me that from his point of view it wasn't over.

Actually we were still in an experimenting phase and even if the new rules, according to the old conception of the Test itself, decreed its end, according to the new awareness that we all reached, they only said one thing: phase 3 was on. The phase in which all that we had learnt allowed us to obtain concrete results finally changing direction to our relationship life, and not only. None of us still knew that this would have been the hardest phase by far. We thought that our improvement allowed us to have an easy life but difficulties were still hard and many. We would have noticed only later. I agreed with John about the promptness of the beginning of phase 3 of the Test and we agreed considering it still alive and not concluded as it would have been if we had discussed with the old rules and old mentality. In fact the spirit of the Test was to discover, experiment and put yourself to the test in a path that would have allowed us to improve our relationship with the opposite sex. From a certain point of view the Test would have never ended. If we had been able to keep this spirit alive, not only we would have obtained better answers but we would have also improved trying to be and obtain more than we ever imagined. The bell rang and I sat down thinking about Chiara and about what she told me a few minutes earlier. In front of me Ilary was sitting with her usual thong coming slightly out of her jeans. I smiled and I had chance to think about something else. It came to my mind that she and Tiffany were still at stake and that I still had to decide how to manage them. I promised myself to decide soon not to find myself in situation worse than the present one. We had Latin for our first hour, subject I didn't love. Nevertheless that morning for at least one hour I didn't find it as futile as usual.

Maybe because I was in a period in which I was appreciating even more what surrounded me (and guess what I was obtaining more than I wanted) or maybe because I still had Chiara's beautiful face in front of me. The point is that we were studying Horace that morning, right that morning, we analysed his well known "Carpe Diem". It was like: "Dum loquimur fugerit invida aetas: carpe diem, quam minimum credula postero." "As we speak time will be gone, as if it hated us. Seize the day, believing the least possible in tomorrow." I couldn't help noticing that the message was so strong despite the hundreds of years that separated it from us. After all, true wisdom has no time. For all the first hour I had chance to think about this concept and how simple yet incredibly charming it was. Exploit any possibility, any single chance that you get without worrying about tomorrow. Living all the way the only moment on which you really have control: present. The past is gone and it will never come back and future is only made of thoughts that we raise today. Don't worry about the future but only focus on today, because the time flows with no rest and every wasted moment is a chance you will not have anymore. I thought about how in the last weeks I had, almost unconsciously, applied this concept to my life and how my life had improved. I spent the last times fully enjoying any opportunity I got with trust and courage, always optimistic about the path I was walking on. Needless to say how much happiness I tasted until now and how much still, I was sure, was awaiting. In my specific case, Chiara now represented the chance I shouldn't have let go. If I hadn't enjoyed my relationship with her I was sure I would have regretted it for all my life. And here my mind went back to the reflection I had already had: how was it possible to be driven by intuition exploiting any chance you could get, without caring about the consequences?

In this case following this strong life philosophy I should enjoyed Chiara. But Giulia would have taken it badly and I wouldn't have felt ok myself doing this. So my question remained. Probably acting only in the present without worrying about tomorrow, in the long term, you would have always been driven to the right direction, obtaining what you needed for your personal growth. But when it comes to interpersonal relationships or respect of other people's feelings I think it would have been devastating. The doubt was tormenting me even if I think that my most rational part was prevailing and it was blocking me on my eternal thinking. What I used to consider the flaw of the old Luke. The paradox could have been that problems actually were rising in that moment you didn't let yourself go in the present, doing what you knew you had to do. "If you let yourself go in any moment without thinking too much, totally free and filled with trust you would have the key to success in your hand." This thought echoed in my head and I realised it was my own instinct to suggest it. All in all it was what I had been doing during the last weeks and that allowed me to reach this new and higher level of awareness. Probably if I had had fun with Chiara, so without going back with Giulia, in the long term, based on the "new me" that I have developed, I would have been happy." My worries were born from my way of thinking which was wrong because pointed towards the past. I should have always acted with my mind pointing towards what I wanted to experiment without hanging to situations and thought from the past.

Since these were holding me, preventing me from growing. If I wanted to change my situation, I had to think with the attitude that I would have had in the moment things actually changed. So I should have hastened with my thought what I wanted and my reality, also acting accordingly, would have then changed. I considered this a great teaching and made it mine. It was easy but not ordinary. Working on the mental method that we had in any occasion was fundamental to anticipate on mental level what wanted to experiment in your own life. "Carpe Diem!" I said to myself. I finished the first hour and Ilary turned to me. And she gave me the chance to test what I had just thought about. "You still haven't told me anything precise about friday night, carpe diem Luke!"

She told me with her usual alluring tone. I couldn't help smiling about how life always put you to the test. Agreeing about the abstract concept of seizing the moment was one thing, but absorbing it making it yours was another. "Ahah I see you were paying attention,..." I replied. Then I added: "Want me to come to the party with you on friday night?" "Yeah... or is there some other girl that invited you?" "Well, could be." I told her, staying blurry, but at the same time aware that all this was just raising my value. "And who invited you? Your ex, Giulia? Or her best friend Chiara? Do you think I didn't see you two arriving together?" "You ask too many questions, my dear Ilary. And you know way too much or you think you know them." I told her with a challenging voice. "Ahah, I know you well Luke and I also know that I'm the last girl that's right for you." She replied, accepting the challenge. "Is that so? Are you sure?" I asked her. "Yes, without a doubt. Maybe you need to have some fun with Chiara to forget Giulia but all in all, at the end of the flirt, you will understand that I'm the one for you." I was intrigued by her self confidence and by what she was saying. In some way she was right but still it wasn't true that I was trying to forget Giulia. And Chiara herself wasn't just a flirt, or at least I thought so. After saying that she turned her back to me. The second hour started and I still had her words echoing in my head. Without a doubt, I had many things to think about lately and I loved accepting all this as a challenge. Given the premise that, however, my intuition would have been in charge. This was my commitment. Too many reflections wouldn't take me anywhere and would have kept me still because any action, potentially, would have had consequences that somehow I couldn't control. But this was part of the game and the objective shouldn't have been controlling everything, but following your inner voice to what would have allowed me to be happy. The spirit of the Test was still alive in me and I was grateful for all I was experimenting; so many chances to enjoy and accept as part of this period full of satisfactions. The rest of the morning flowed away with no particular worries; after all, I think that not much could equal the impact that "carpe diem" had on me during the first hour. During the break I met the little Tiffany in the courtyard and I took the chance to spend a few words with her. She came to me anyway and like Ilary a few hours before she pointed out that I still hadn't given her an answer about friday night. Anyway she didn't look exasperated and I thought that this fear was still a leftover from the past; the "old Luke" would have never left a girl's invitation pending for the fear to lose it. Now I really know that looking busy and elusive gave me great value and was making me much more attractive to the girls' eyes, allowing me to indulge before I could give them an answer. The good thing was that I consciously didn't project outside the image that was now perceived; I intentionally didn't put effort in trying to look in some way so that I could have more chances and be more desired. I was completely natural in my behaviour and this proved that I got the hang of a way of living which was particularly winning and at the same time it felt appropriate for me. Not bad, given that a few weeks earlier the situation was completely different. I realised that Tiffany didn't really feel like talking and I didn't mind that, after all. We withdrew behind a corner away from indiscreet eyes, and we kissed as if we hadn't seen each other for long time. My self esteem lately was reaching values never seen before and it was now rising to unmatched heights. At a certain point Tiffany stopped and said: "You know Luke, I missed you. I really wanted to see you..." She was staring at me with her beautiful eyes making me feel really good. We kept kissing way past break time, but we didn't notice immediately. I noticed how late it was but Tiffany didn't seem to care. "Darn it's so late, let's get back to class!" I exclaimed, maybe giving her the idea to be a swot (nothing farther from the truth...). "Why? Are you in a hurry?" Tiffany asked me, standing still in total quiet. "Break time ended half an hour ago!" I told her, trying to make her understand the gravity of it. "Ahah, fine we can go back to class." She answered. I went back to the class and excused my delay giving the excuse that the school representatives needed me; an excuse that I had already used in the past and that had always proven itself effective. As soon as I sat down, Ilary gave me a note saying: "I know where you really were." And that worried me not because she had seen me with Tiffany, provided it was true, but because I felt like I was spied on. Then I laughed because it sounded pretty much like a second rate horror movie message. I spent the rest of the morning on Facebook checking the comments that the guys were posting on the page that we created at the beginning of the Test. They all agreed on the passage to phase 3 right now. We wanted more freedom thanks to which we could give value to what we learnt so far and now it was really time to change the rules again so that the Test could keep helping us. It wasn't over then as someone thought. It only evolved and its principles were still as lively as ever. I was glad to see that all the guys were particularly appreciating how John and I managed the experiment so far; the good thing was that we shared, until now, a common project aimed to provide us with starting ideas to improve ourselves. All the guys abode the rules and the general mood had always been high, sign that the vision of the reason why we did this was clear from the beginning. Furthermore all the guys in school wisely exploited this situation to work on themselves and improve as never before. The path I was taking, I realised, was the same as many others. Each of them was different, had his personal story, his qualities but we were all joined by this personal improvement that within a few weeks allowed us to know ourselves better and to improve a lot obtaining enjoyable results. This has obviously favoured the respect for the rules that in turn had supported this "self work" in a positive spiral from which we were all taking benefits. In a certain way, even the fact that we had started, together with John this extremely positive "mass" phenomenon, made me feel godly because whether we wanted it or not, John and I were innovators and reference points for many guys that every day were asking us for advice. "What's better in life than improving yourself and becoming inspiration for other people engaged in the same path!" I proudly thought. The sound of the bell decreed the end of the day and before I could leave the room, Ilary stopped me to talk: it was only me and her in the classroom. "You know Luke, I don't care if you're dating other girls lately. I only want to be with you. I want you to understand I'm the right one." She said, repeating what she had told me earlier. I found her self confident and sexy as usual, so I decided to meet with her that same afternoon: "I understand that. This afternoon I'm busy but I can find an hour to spare to see you." "It would be cool..." She replied with a bright face. "Come to my place at 6. I'm home alone." I told her, making her understand we could have some fun. "Ok, see you later." She simply said. She gave me one last mischievous look and then she set out for the exit. I left the room and found Chiara in the hallway and it looked like she was waiting for me.

"Hi Luke, how was your morning?" She asked me, but a big smile on her beautiful face. "All standard, no fireworks." For a moment I wondered if she was asking that because she had seen me with Tiffany during the break. It wasn't like that. "And how was yours?" I asked her almost automatically. "Fine, even if I missed you." She replied in a very sweet way. I felt rewarded for what she said and the dilemma that was gripping me came back to my mind; after studying Horace's "Carpe Diem" during the first hour things had only tangled.

It looked like Chiara was putting some effort in making my life complicated even if a part of me was really appreciating her considerations towards me. "Do you feel like riding me home?" She asked. How could I say no? Those sweet eyes of hers were demanding affection and I couldn't reject it. I smiled, maybe also blushing a bit because after all this searching from her embarrassed me a bit. And I didn't know why. "Did you blush? How sweet..." She said smiling. "It's ok, I'll give you a ride home" I told her, trying to hide my emotions. "Great!" She said, kissing me on the cheek. We arrived to the courtyard and most of the guys had already left. I loaded her on the Vespa and I headed to her house. I enjoyed how she was hugging my hips while we were dashing through the traffic. With all this girls loading on my Vespa, I always had a second helmet with me. It was handy by now. When we got to her house with things going the way they were I realised she had no intention of letting me go so easily. In fact she asked me if I wanted to stay for lunch. But I had promised myself from during the trip from school to Chiara's that I would have dropped her and said goodbye right away to avoid further involvement before I could make my ideas clear. But things were going differently. I was determined to refuse her invitation but nevertheless my mouth let a "fine" slip out!" I ended up locking my Vespa and having lunch at her place. She was home alone because her parents were at work so I enjoyed cooking, making lunch and giving the idea of someone who could cook. It wasn't absolutely like that, but I enjoyed doing it and however as I had already noticed, it left an impression on girls. Even if the last thing I wanted now was to further heat things up. She really appreciated my cooking skills and somehow I felt that now we were as close as ever. Even if being close was making everything less controllable. But also terribly exciting. Once had lunch my inner voice awoke again whispering, or I should say screaming, to leave to avoid getting in trouble again. I couldn't listen to it. My resistance, once again, were falling. We sat on her bed and Chiara reached out for me in a very affectionate way. For a moment I thought maybe she didn't want to do it; after all she cared for Giulia and I really don't think she wanted to betray her trust again. Maybe the only fact that we were together was enough, aware at the same time that we couldn't go further. We talked and joked for some time and I must say that the atmosphere was really pleasant. She was really an extraordinary girl and even the only fact that I was there with her was really delightful. "This morning you looked quite sad when we got to school." I told her. There was a moment of silence, then she replied: "Yeah, I was sad." She said without saying anything else.

"Are you feeling better now?" I asked her. "Now I am. But if I can't be with you, if can't make love to you. I will never be truly happy." She said, giving me a kiss on the lips. "I understand, I am torn as well. But I don't want to cheat on Giulia again." "Neither do I. But what I feel for you is too strong." Chiara replied. I could perfectly feel what she was feeling and it was clear that the most natural thing would have been to let ourselves go. We would have both gained great benefit. Passion was really strong and suppressing it would have been harmful. What I learnt in the last weeks was really the importance of letting yourself go, to follow your instinct with courage, conscious that this would have been the road to happiness.

But a part of me was holding me back for respect to Giulia. I was still in love with Giulia and I didn't want her to feel bad. Least of all, doing it with Chiara and hide it from her. The situation was pretty complicated. With Chiara next to me I really didn't know how the afternoon would have ended. I wanted to kiss her until I wore her out but I couldn't. At some point the bell rang and Chiara told me that Giulia and Camilla arrived. This might have been the confirmation that she didn't mean to have sex with me and that her rational part was prevailing too that was telling her to stop. I wondered how Giulia would have reacted if she saw me at Chiara's.

CHAPTER 19

LOVE THEM ALL

The four of us gathered in the living room and for the first time I had the chance to spend some time with Camilla even if we were not alone. Some time before I set to myself I wanted to get to know her better but then I stopped because of the recent dilemma of the relationship with Chiara. Camilla was really cute and honestly I wanted to go out with her, even just once to know what kind of chick she was. But the first thing I had to do was understanding deeply what I felt for Chiara and how to manage the relationship. The choice I would have made was not clear. In that living room with those 3 hot girls I was really feeling great. I realized that my problem was that I was secretly in love with all those gorgeous girls who I was relating to. In that room I couldn't keep myself from noticing the beauty of them all and I couldn't hide the fact that I felt a kind of attraction for each one of them. I posed on the thought that just came up in my mind.

"Am I really in love with all the nice girls I stumble in? Or is it just a sensation which doesn't mean anything? Maybe it's not necessarily love but physical attraction..." Actually few days before I composed a song whose title was: "Love 'em all" and I uploaded it on my site: www. LucaGrisendiArt.com

After all, if someone asked me to choose one of the three, I couldn't answer immediately. Giulia was the one who I had the deepest relation with and what I felt for her was stronger than my feelings for the others. But I was extremely attracted by Chiara and I felt the need to know better Camilla. I started wondering if it was normal or not to feel attraction toward so many girls at the same time. "I wondered how they could react if they knew..." While they were chatting and doing a little bit of gossip, I couldn't keep myself dreaming about the 4 of us in a nice king side bed freeing our teenagers physical instincts. Doing it with 3 girls at the same time would have been simply incredible but even hard, I thought smiling. Camilla asked me why I was smiling and Giulia and Chiara turned to me curiously. "Nothing." I answered without hiding my amusement. Obviously this thing made the curiosity grow. "Come on, why are you laughing?" They asked me all together and everything started becoming damn fun. "Who? Me? Not laughing." I answered fomenting the excitement.

"Come one, you tell us!" Camilla said with a sweated voice and added: "Giuly, Chiara, you keep him, now he has to tell us." Giulia and Chiara came near me one for a side on the sofa where I was lying and the whole thing started looking very similar to my fantasy. I was feeling something between fun and excitement. Moving and touching on the sofa, even just for fun, with Chiara, Giulia and Camilla who came after them, was quite nice. And extremely fun. Three gorgeous girls who were almost rubbing on me were making that afternoon very interesting. Giulia didn't ask why I was at Chiara's and the general mood was quite high. Actually I was quite high. The old Luke couldn't even dream about this kind of experience. We were just joking but we could get close to my fantasies very soon. Even because what I learned was that to get any results the first and most important thing was to believe in it strongly from the beginning and I wanted to believe. We kept joking for a while and getting to a pillow battle we had crazy fun. I realized how you could really have fun with girls without involving sex. It was quite of a new for me. And extremely positive new for me. After playing we calmed down a little bit and nobody realized that I didn't answered to the question. They all had the hair messed up and they were extremely sexy. My fantasy has been fueled up now and I felt that chances to make it become real were growing. Or maybe I was just crazy but I didn't care. After the personal growth that I lived in the last few weeks, I didn't want to impose myself any limit. More than ever now that I had the chance to make an unforgettable experience. Around mid afternoon Chiara, Giulia and Camilla started watching girly tv series which I could never ever watch. This is what I thought immediately. But after I forced myself to stay there trying not to judge and trying to understand what they were finding so exciting in those series. Even if I couldn't stand them in the beginning, if I could get to understand why girls liked them so much, I could evolve in my relationship with the other sex. Understanding their tastes better, I could understand them deeper and I could be ready to get better results than before. Anyway this was a new and original way to live the situation and grow personally. It could have been fun or maybe at the end I would have started liking tv series that they watched. What I really cared, actually, was testing always myself to grow over and over; seeing those 3 beautiful girls I was feeling inside me the will to take the best out of every single occasion of fun and pleasure time with them. I thought I was establishing a new virtuous circle inside of me that was pushing me to find always new challenges: in the past I always avoided this kind of experience. Obviously this was very difficult but at the same time incredibly efficient in term of payback I could get. So I spent the rest of the afternoon watching those tv series with them while chatting on facebook with John telling him about the 3 chicks I had in front of me. Our comments and our considerations were many and obvious. At the end I thought that tv series we were watching were a lot less horrible than I thought. "I supposed this is what happens every time you try not to judge and you open yourself to something new: you discover that it is not absolutely the way you thought so you always have the chance to learn something useful. After all life itself is a sum of experiences and if you exclude a lot only because you have prejudices, you lose a lot of occasions of self-enrichment." I thought. What they were watching was full of love stories and extremely focused on personal and relationships. Girls, and this was not a new, were a lot more sensitive to feelings and their expression inside a relationship. The gap from boys was very wide but this didn't mean it was impossible to understand them and build a satisfactory relationship with them. Excluding the pure physical element. And this to me was a challenge. At the end of the afternoon, after I wrote down my notes and my observations to improve my relationship with girls based on what they liked, I took Giulia home and this time she had the seat on my Vespa. As soon as we arrived, she asked if I wanted to join for dinner. I though that it as a good idea mainly because I could talk to her about what I was feeling for Chiara. I thought that this was the only way to solve the problem or maybe to try to solve it. It could be risky but I couldn't see any other chance at the moment. There weren't many other options or anyhow trying to being open and sincere to Giulia would have been the best and most honest thing for her. I would have explained to her how much I was attracted by Chiara but that at the same time I didn't want to see her suffer. I was hoping she would have understood me even if I didn't really know how she would react and what solution we could find. On one side, I wanted to keep everything simply the way it was. The more diplomatic and wise part of me was always pushing me to find the best solution for everyone, something which could meet everyone's needs. But in this case, as in all similar cases, someone would have been hurt. At least I wanted to limit the damage and I thought that honesty would have paid me back, somehow. I told Giulia ok and I stayed over for dinner. Her family was there and we had dinner all together. Her parents were very nice, with a young spirit. I enjoyed everything and her mother was a great cook. After dinner, we went upstairs to her bedroom and as soon as we shut the door, Giulia jumped on me. We started kissing passionately and we laid down on her bed in a very hot way. What I wanted to tell her about Chiara moved to the background and without even realizing it, we were naked, making love, as we didn't see each other for ages.

Actually, I really needed that and everything was even more satisfying because she took the initiative. I started thinking about her parents could hear us but I didn't care after all. They were surely conscious of what was going on in their daughter bedroom. After the passion, it was time for my "speech". She was beautiful, laying on her bed, with her hair covering the whole pillow. I wasn't sure that was the right time but I thought: the sooner the better, in this case.

"Giulia, there is something I need to tell you." Hoping to find the right way to tell her. "Sure, go ahead." She answered, giving me whole her attention.

Her face was spreading joy and her big blue eyes were shining more than ever before. I was afraid I would have ruined this moment but I kept on talking.

After a moment of silence I started: "It has something to do with Chiara..." I anticipated and I could immediately see her eyes loosing tranquillity and joy.

"After I apologized with you the other day, I never slept with her again. I have too much respect for you and I don't want to hurt you anymore..." "So, what's wrong?" She asked. "The fact is that I'm attracted to Chiara and I feel that a part of me would like to go forward with her..." "What do you mean? Are you in love with her?" "No I don't think so. It is pure physical attraction but I'm forcing myself to resist and I don't know how to behave. I don' want to hurt you but I can't hide every time I see her, I can't consider her just as a friend. What I feel is a lot stronger..." "This means that when you slept with her you were already feeling something for her..." She said. "I don't know. Let's say I realized it in these last few days and I decided to tell you because I couldn't find an answer or a solution to this situation." I told her, trying to make her understand that I cared for her feelings. And I kept: "You know me and you know I always try to find the right solution for everybody but it is something difficult this time."

I didn't know what her reaction could have been. I wished my honesty would have helped me but anyhow, that's what I did, try to be honest.

"I understand or think I do. I I thought we would have got back together soon but I realize you are still confused. You've got to make your own decisions Luke, I'm in love with you and knowing you are attracted to Chiara hurts me of course. I'm afraid I'm gonna lose you." She said kind of sad. This convinced me the solution didn't exist. Or, I had to choose between her and Chiara and suffer the consequences of my choice. There was no magic solution and no way out. I thought I could have got everything but that was not possible. "I decided to tell you because I think that the best thing now is to be honest with you. We can't get back together if I don't make up my mind, before." Giulia seemed worried. She was deeply in love with me, she had always been. Even when she left me and even after I cheated on her with Chiara. She forgave me. She was afraid I could leave her definitively and start dating Chiara. I was confused but I knew something: what I felt for Giulia was very strong and even though I liked Chiara, I could never feel the same for her. If I had gone back with Giulia I would have missed my relation with Chiara; plus they were friends so I would have seen Chiara for a long time, anyway. Useless keeping thinking. I had to take my decision. "I will never feel what I feel for you, with Chiara. You are so special to me and I feel that this is my place, here with you." I was surprised my self saying those words considering all my doubts. My deep feeling were screaming that Giulia was the right one for me in that moment, covering superficials thoughts' noise. "Happy to hear this from you." Said Giulia and she added unexpectedly: "Want you again, now." I smiled. Useless to reaffirm how pure passion could expressed our feeling better than anything. I spent the night over. I could feel she was the right girl for me. And I slept on it.

CHAPTER 20

WE HAVE TO BE ABLE TO CHOOSE

Tuesday, October the 18th

I woke up the next morning and as soon as I opened my eyes, I saw Giulia's features highlighted by sun rays coming from the window. I couldn't wake up in a better way. Even before I could start talking, she kissed me deeply. I wanted to stay there in the bed with her all day long. I received a message from John which interrupted the atmosphere. He was saying that he has important news for me regarding the Test and he wanted to talk to me. I had breakfast with Giulia, I took her to school and then I went to my high-school. As soon as I got there I met John in the school-yard and he told me we had one hour free so that we could update on phase 3 of the Test. This was a great way to distract me from "Giulia & Chiara" dilemma. Guess what, I wrote a song about it called: "Giulia&Chiara" (www. LucaGrisendiArt.com). Old John told me even if phase 3 started at the right moment, things were not going the way we talk. Many guys were capitalizing the past growth but results were not that great. We didn't know the reason for this. We probably overvalued things or maybe we just had to wait a few days to have some information we could work on. Anyway, the guys from our school were not reporting anything positive. It was difficult to come to conclusions with just a few cases and we didn't know much about them. The guys had a hard time fixing appointments with girls and this wasn't making any sense. Things did go very well till now and each of us had the chance to improve our relation with the opposite sex. We started our adventure because we weren't satisfied but now we improved obtaining great results. Things had to go better. In the first phase of the Test, when rules were extremely severe, we understood our mistakes in our approach with girls so we decided to loosen our limitations in order to have more informations. We were in phase three now and if we were lucky we would have had great satisfactions. But girls still seemed not collaborate. Clearly, we still had something to learn and I felt that this would have been the toughest step. Everything we did till now was not enough and we still needed to put everything into question and reinvent ourselves in order to understand what our mistakes were. Sadness immediately changed into the clear will to persevere despite difficulties, looking for results. I started thinking about girls again, about what I experienced at Chiara's when Giulia, Camilla and her were watching girls-series o Tv. I started thinking that we had always focalized our attention on ourselves, on our self growth and on our way to relate to girls. It wasn't completely wrong as results told us. But now it was time for focusing on girls: we had to know and understand them better. Exactly what I did when I watched girls tv series with Chiara Giulia and Camilla: watch them, live their tastes to get to know them better. We grew and improved ourselves a lot and this was just great. We understood many things about ourselves and how to relate better with the opposite sex. This was a fact: but it wasn't enough anymore. Phase three would have really stressed our motivation and our will to "really go for it" all the way. I was sure that that the other guys wanted to go on: not only for the results we had till now but also for the will to keep going till the end. We were running our world race and we couldn't pull back now. This phase wouldn't have probably been easier that the others before; we had a clear picture of what we could achieve from this Test as we didn't at the beginning of it. I shared this thought with John, Robert, Jack and Simon who were there in that moment; they shared my feeling and my ideas. Thanks to my intuition the only thing to do was follow it! But I needed nerve to follow my intuition because I was forced to go out my comfort zone and to live "uncomfortable" situations. As usual, nothing revolutionary. We were understanding how much we improved ourselves knowing, now, what we had to do, what path we had to follow. In phases one and two we understood what wasn't going the right way only when the problem was already there, real. In that moment we were forced by circumstances. Now we anticipated and forecasted everything: phase three started before the guys even asked us and we already knew how to manage it. We felt better knowing we could face everything faithfully and bravely. We had those characteristics and we took them out lately. We had to concentrate our efforts and attention on girls without focalizing on the final result too much since it could have moved us from what we wanted. If we had approached girls without thinking of what we "actually" wanted, we wouldn't have obtained concrete results. This meant enjoying relating with girls verbally before trying any physical approach. We had to consider that the physical was a question mark, nothing sure: the main point was to build satisfactory relationships from the beginning without thinking "about that" all the time. This new approach would have let us know the girl better, having a real relationship with her apart from sex. A more mature and complex relation that would have helped us understanding the opposite sex better. Consequently, if we had came to the point to relating to all girls in a mature and satisfactory way, we could change the single approach in the right way in different situations. Maybe, with some girls, we would have built a simple friendship and it would have been natural and safe. This was possible now that we had a lot more opportunities and we had the chance to choose who we wanted to go deeper with. We took everything it came in the past, because we didn't have other choices. We weren't creating opportunities and occasions were lived without the chance to know if we really wanted them or not. We were now to the point we could choose: the objective was to manage and handle the relationships with girls so that we could choose the one we really feel we had a special connection with. But we had to open up with them giving them the chance to know us better and make the relationship real and clear. We were all feeling the same, we were together in this intention and need. I laughed thinking that we had thought for a second the Test could end: the Test was alive! More alive then ever! The first hour off had been very interesting and profitable: we understood quickly what was the path we had to follow and we decided to communicate everything to our schoolmates (guys of course). As usual they shared and agreed with us and results obtained proved what John and I were constantly sharing on the Test facebook page. We were suggesting what we had to work on and our credibility, after the results, was extreme. This made us happy. John and I and the other guys got back to classes to start a new school morning; we had already posted our new consideration and comments were coming fast one after the other. I think that the support from the other guys from the school came from the indications John and I were constantly giving, being a guiding light for everyone. This was even making things easier. Knowing what to do, we immediately started working to save precious time. We were all very excited and we all wanted to go on in this nice and constructive "journey". The morning passed without dramatic events and the bell time came pretty soon. As I got to the school yard I saw Chiara talking to Giulia; obviously Giulia finished a little before in her school and came by to meet with us. They saw me, smiled at me calling me over. For one second I thought where Tiffany was: I would have called her later on. And I thought that if I had called her, that would have been the first time I contacted her and not viceversa. Seeing Giulia and Chiara together was making me feel strange: the blond and the brunette, my girlfriend and my lover, the wildest, Chiara and the quite one, Giulia. "Was the really no chance to have fun with both?" I thought halfway seriously. I repeated myself that considering the new developments, the new "Luke" didn't have and want to have limits. So I kept that fantasy clear in my mind, sure that one day it could have happened. I liked that challenge and I know I was the only one it could make it happen. "Hi girls, you look great today, are you excited for the weekend? I told them. They were really beautiful together, sexier than ever. "Excited for the pajama party! You are going to be there, right?" Answered Chiara, named the "Party animal". Thinking about having both at the party, with loud music and limitless alcoholics, was quite exciting. Even too exciting. Saturday was a holiday so that friday night would have been the top night of the week and of the month. The party was taking place at a guy from the school's place, american stile and we all knew were going to have a "real party" that night. I had to manage Giulia and Chiara plus Tiffany and Ilary with who I didn't know what would have happened. Everything was madly crazy but I was waiting for that night to come. "Of course I'll be there! Are you going to be the same old party animal?" I answered Chiara, joking. "Uh Uh, who me a party animal? I'm a quite girl, even to quite..." She replied a little embarrassed. Giulia told me they were going out for lunch and she asked if I wanted to join them. "Of course" I thought. I noticed how she wasn't showing to much attention to my attraction for Chiara, she was even inviting me for lunch with them. This is what I loved of Giulia: she was a concrete girl who wasn't making no drama. She was just making me crazy; in someway she was the perfect girlfriend. We had lunch together and I was there with two beautiful girls joking and laughing like crazy. I was happy too see that despite we were all living strong emotions the mood was high and relaxed at the same time. There was no tension at all and I thought that ironically my dream was coming true. If I had started thinking logically as I had done before I would have been even more confused. I decided not to try to understand everything in every moment every time. A rational answer was too difficult to find, anyway, and I had realized that intuition was the best guide to happiness. This had represented one of my biggest limits in the past: analyzing every detail, understanding and controlling everything. If I had to think about my life I should have left it to pure intuition and not to analysis and rational schemes. It was terribly difficult but necessary at the same time, for my personal growth. Control was a weakness because it took a good confidence to let yourself go. And I got this self confidence slowly during the last weeks feeling it was growing. Deep inside of me I knew I was everything I wanted to be and I had everything I wanted to have; it was just a question of self confidence which helped taking out all my strengths. Giulia and Chiara saw me lost in my thoughts (as usual) and interrupted my mental trip: "Hello Luke, are you there? What are thinking about?" Asked Chiara. "Nothing..." I replied quickly. "All right, I know what you were thinking..." She said. "Ok, so what was I thinking?" I answered, understanding Chiara was warming up the air, as usual. "Well, Giulia and I were talking about where to sleep friday night after the party. Maybe you were dreaming about this". I honestly hadn't even heard that part of their dialogue, lost in my thoughts. But thinking about it, now, this was quite interesting. I immediately stopped from thinking why Giulia seemed not to care about my attraction towards Chiara. Even because this was *my* feeling. She was probably worried inside. The way Chiara was acting and talking half joking was exciting me very much. From this point of view she was a lot more "modern than" Giulia. "Well, who knows. It could be.." I told her, looking straight in her eyes. Giulia jumped in saying "No, it can't be. Luke loves only me!" She said showing her feelings. I could feel that she said that just to calm her self down and in that moment I understood how strong was what she felt for me. She put my hand on mine. I liked how Giulia could be sweet and tender, making you know how much you meant for her. I thought that invite for lunch wasn't meaningless: Giulia came to our school, after lesson to invite Chiara out for lunch sure that I was going to join them. Doing this she wanted to demonstrate that I was "engaged" and that our relationship was too strong to be destroyed. I don't really now if Giulia had talked with Chiara about what I told her about my attraction for her friend. Maybe not and now she was communicating to her without using word. If I had got it, I was sure Chiara got the message herself clear and nice. I watched Giulia in her blue big eyes. When she was showing her love for me that way, I could feel her as "THE ONLY GIRL IN THE WORLD", as Rihanna sang. We kept on joking as we were three simple friends. It was nice staying there with them and for the first time, or so, I started appreciating girls presence without thinking about something more. This is what we had to work in this third phase of the Test: building real and strong relationships with girls without immediately thinking about sex. What a challenge! As we noticed, anyway, this was the best way to succeed. Only having a good relation with girls we could get to the point where, if really in interested", sex would have been a natural consequence. It was important to underline "if really interested": with a better confidence we had to live more occasion as possible in order to be able to choose the one we really wanted. This was something we couldn't even imagine in the past. After lunch, we walked to Chiara's house where Camilla would have met us, to double the afternoon before. I wasn't studying anymore and I couldn't remember where I lived but that was ok. The energy in the air, with Camilla there, would have been good and high and I was ready to move my attention from the attraction to girls to analysis and deep understanding. Of course during the afternoon few fantasies me by my head but I wouldn't have given to much attention to them. I was very serious about my project, the Test, from the very beginning and I felt to do what was right and necessary instead of what was easy. Spending entire afternoons with three beautiful girls was clearly the best way to do something I would have never done in the past, at the same time trying to learn how to relate better with girls. What I wanted to do wasn't so obvious: I didn't think about how we was relating to other people that much and how we could do it better. With the Test, we all reached higher levels of consciousness and I really wanted to go on that way. I also realized that the process improvements wouldn't have stopped, and that the Test itself represented the beginning of a new phase that would have never stopped with the end of the Test. This project was a new way of thinking, a new approach we had built and that was still in progress. I didn't know if some other crazy guys existed, guys that gave themselves a challenge to improve their relationship with girls. We had been always pushed by improvisation in picking up girls. Maybe some guys were already good in relating to girls while others weren't but no one was asking himself if he could improve. We all discovered the limitless potential and until we had results we would have kept going on. Giulia, Chiara and Camilla started gossiping and I started chatting with John on my iPad. Our daily updates on the Test were extremely important and useful: a lot of benefits which came from the project came from our confronting with each other talking about our feelings, sharing our considerations. In that moment I thought about the three beautiful girls there in Chiara's living room completely unaware, like all the girls of our high school, of the Test. But this wasn't something new. It was incredible they didn't even heard about it and that they didn't suspect anything, most of all in the beginning when rules imposed us to behave in a particular way. I myself was chatting with John on the Test with the three girls talking with each other. I smiled thinking that the top-secret project was on its way since weeks. This aspect itself made everything very exciting because it was like living in a movie and actually it really was that way! I could have thought that gossip was something stupid but I started thinking that this behavior showed that girls were more focused on human feelings and personal relations between young people than guys (did). Girls were more focalized on intercourses between people and they cared more about feeling involved. It wasn't something new that girls were more sensitive and emotional than us but the more interesting thing was interested in relations that didn't involve them personally in a way which could seem almost obsessive. They were spending hour and hours talking how they (o their girlfriends) acted in this or that way, and why she related that way, etc.. They were far different from our way of behaving and on what they were concentrating on the emotional part of a relationship on what they were feeling, while we were a lot more "simple". A lot less complicated. If I (and then the other guys from the school) could concentrate on understanding a "woman's worth" I would have taken everyone to a different level which could give us much more satisfaction. This was the phase three's goal. We weren't having the best results because of the lack of listening. We were approaching them without paying any real attention to what they were communicating. This is why we didn't have satisfactory relationships. Communication problems: until now we though that showing an attitude was enough to succeed but we were finding out that this wasn't the most important quality a guy should have. Chatting with John we came to a conclusion: listening what was girls need and were asking for. After all this was a necessary characteristic in every human relation. Very clear, theoretically. Practical test would have been more difficult. In that moment, while I was listening to the beautiful girls there with me talking, I understood that sex differences made everything difficult: I myself was quite bored by their gossip after all. But I wasn't paying enough attention and I wasn't going deeper. Now I knew what was the aspect I had to work on and I forced myself to suspend any judgment and try to know their tastes and the reason of them. It was quite an effort but I had motivation and modesty enough to make it. It could have even be exciting. I started being fascinated by how long they could talk about this or that relation, always underline the emotional aspect. From my guy point of view, this was completely unusual.

CHAPTER 21

A DIFFERENT NIGHT

We were at the end of October and it was very cold even I had no problems with low temperatures. I remember all of a sudden about weather forecasts saying that it would have snowed and actually the sky from my window looked "nervous". It started snowing soon and hard. I realized it was impossible to drive my Vespa. Slippery wheels: suicide. "My" girls told me not to risk anything on the streets; typical maternal instinct and behavior that I really liked. Now that I was getting to know girls better, even outside the sheets, I could notice aspects I didn't know about them. It was late afternoon and we received a call from Chiara's parents from the house on the hills nearby: they've got there in the morning and they didn't feel to take the car back to town so, surprise, surprise, it was just us, the girls and I, at Chiara's. I couldn't leave because of my Vespa and the snow, Giulia came with me and Camilla decided to just stay without asking her parents to come and pick her up with that bad weather and the traffic jam. The situation was electrifying and I felt that the night would have been quite interesting. The Test started a real revolution in my life. I could have never imagined I would have found my self in a house with three beautiful girls, with a snowstorm. The adventure spell was strong and I realized that I was the one who really changed. The Test just forced me from the very beginning to change my point of view on many things. I even realized I was now living an interesting and fulfilling life. And I was feeling goooooood! We were stuck in the house, so I asked Chiara if we had enough food for the night. I opened the fridge and everything was there. I decided to cook, just to act as a good guy who can cook knowing this was making quite an impression. I made fish and the result was good and I had fun too; me and the girls joked all the time, they helped me and I had a great time. I was telling them what to take, how to prepare it and honestly this was one the best evenings of my life. And this without any physical approach. Having such fun without having sex wasn't an obvious thing to me. Not till that night. My life was opening new and nice experiences shaking my little world and my certainties were falling apart. I enjoyed leaving those old thoughts. I was feeling free and so good. We had a nice dinner drinking a good white wine from Chiara father's cellar down in the basement. I knew girls would have got drunk and as I predicted they were pretty high after just few glasses. I liked it. Actually I didn't feel uncomfortable with it. The evening would have been even more interesting and unpredictable. After dinner, Chiara, push by the alcohol level in her blood, opened her father's liquors' cabinet. "Hey your father must be an alcoholic!" I shouted, joking. The cabinet was full of different liquors I'm sure the girls had never tasted before. There was an alcoholics chess Giulia gave Chiara for her birthday. I grabbed it and push by the excitement I asked them to play. The atmosphere was unreal: three girls almost drunk ready to play it dangerously. My dreams about Chiara and Giulia together wasn't far from reality, I thought. And Camilla was there too. We opened the box and started the game; I didn't know how to play and I knew I was loosing my mental alertness. Girls were not geniuses as well, so games were pretty well-balanced. The general energy was extremely high and we were laughing so hard: not bad for a Tuesday night. We were sitting on the carpet, leaning on the sofa. All of a sudden Chiara stood up, turned the stereo on playing my song I had on line on my site: www.LucaGrisendiArt.com. The situation was getting really crazy and I liked it. The chess drove us to the next level; we were out of control and I was ready for everything to happen. I thought that was the wonderful consequence of the Test; I didn't know it before but I opened a new life for me full of incredible experiences. I couldn't describe what I was living. But I was about to discover it. The best was about to come. The music was pumping and Chiara started dancing wild while Camilla and I were trying to play. Giulia was quite drunk and she joined Chiara. We were singing and laughing loudly, feeling free and happy. This is the way teens should be, I thought. Despite the noise and confusion I realized how much we had drunk. A lot.

Chiara and Giulia wanted to wear a pigiama in order to feel more comfortable. They ran upstairs and I kept trying to play chess with Camilla but she kissed me, out of the blue. Considering how drunk I was and the fact that she was very cute...well, I started losing all my inhibitions. I didn't even think about Giulia could get downstairs in a moment. We kissed more and more hard till Giulia and Chiara's stepping down forced Camilla to stop. She had a gorgeous face and that kiss was incredibly deep. Chiara and Giulia were in their pigiamas looking even more sexy than before to me. I always liked girls in their casual suits or pajamas even more than in night, party-dresses. They were still high and they didn't see Camilla's kiss. I could see she wanted me more. The situation was crazy and we were drunk and wild. Music was still pumpin' and the atmosphere was getting hotter and hotter; Giulia sat near me and started kissing me while Chiara and Camilla kept playing chess. Giulia was wilder after drinking and we started kissing passionately on the sofa. We were about to have sex in front of the two other girls. The door bell rang. Giulia and I stopped and Chiara went to the door, trying to keep straight. The old lady from the house near was asking if everything was ok. Giulia, Camilla and I started laughing: the scene was so funny! Chiara herself almost laughed in the old lady's face while reassuring her we were ok. We went back to the sofa and while Chiara turned the music back on Giulia and I started rolling on the sofa. They were seriously drunk and I was surprised they could keep drinking while playing. While Giulia was lying on me, Chiara started touching my butt. We were all pretty wild and while Giulia was completely "rubbed" on me, Chiara laid on the sofa beside me and started touching my butt. I couldn't really understand if I was dreaming or not, but, I tell you, If that was dream, I wanted to keep on sleeping for EVER. Giulia seemed not to care, I could even feel her hotter. Without thinking too long, I put my hand on Chiara's "marble" butt encouraging her to have fun with us. My greatest fantasy was getting real and I wanted to enjoy it. I knew that situation couldn't be easily repeatable. After all she just kissed me and she wouldn't stayed there looking at us. Camilla wasn't here yet. I started thinking about how many coincidences drove me there, on that sofa with two girls on me and a third one almost ready. Obviously I knew these were not coincidences even if some events were not under my control. For example, the snow. Giulia kept ignoring Chiara and things were getting really hot. The all three of us were completely wild now. Passion and pure attraction were now ending to a strong physical approach which could not be stopped by any rational thought. We were instinct-driven we couldn't stop anymore. In everyday life rational behaviors would have won and our limits and our fears would have kept us from express what we had deep inside. But now it was different and we liked it. Giulia and Chiara started taking their clothes off and thank God for that moment I was living. Everything I always asked for was now happening in whole its magnificence. I couldn't explain it to myself but I didn't care. It was time to turn off my brain and leave pure emotions drive me. My dear instinct drove me there and I finally realized that was the right way. Giulia and Chiara were completely naked now and I was so excited I was totally out of control. The girls were, as well. First time for me with two girls in that context and I can say there wasn't better pleasure. Two naked girls, over me, with Get Down pumpin', this was something I would have never forget. I couldn't say who was the hottest and both gave their best in this occasion. Chiara, as I noticed before, was the wildest but Giulia was nothing less. While they were taking my clothes off, Camilla joined us, almost naked. I was really dreaming. This experience confirmed to myself once again that the cody language was extremely more effective in emotions transfer and sharing; at the same time it was clear that I had to make these occasions happen more often. Most of the times, unfortunately, fear stopped us from express our instincts. In this case we let what we had inside to show and we were living unforgettable pleasure moments. I did my best because managing the three girls together was quite an effort but the emotional density made me draw my resource I din't know I had. In the latest weeks I had the chance to start being in the running and leave my comfort zone but in this situation I was going further beyond what I thought it was possible. I thought making love with Giulia and Chiara together was just a dream but it had become just true, it was even better; Camilla joined us and excitement was crazy. The high music in the living room covered girls pleasure moanings and I think nobody could believe that scene was real. This was the best thing I have ever done and pleasure was beyond words. The three girls were all very wild as they had similar experiences before. I couldn't exclude that possibility but I think this was the first time in this context as it was for me. Anyway they seemed comfortable and I liked that considering that Giulia and I were "together" someway. Nothing was clear at this point. We had been overwhelmed by emotions. After having fun together, we all fell asleep, thanks to the drinks too. We had a deep and good sleep till late in the morning. I woke up around 11.30 am.

Wednesday October the 19th

As I opened my eyes, I needed a few minutes to understand where I was and what had happened. I saw Giulia, Chiara and Camilla laying on me, beside me and I realized it had not been a dream. A big smile appeared on my face and just enjoyed what I had lived. I couldn't believe it. But it was real and those three girls on the bed where the proof I lived my dreams, even beyond what I thought it was possible. They were still sleeping and I didn't move not to wake them up, staring their beauty and thanking myself. I needed to pinch myself to believe that the night before I had most incredible experience in my life. I couldn't think of what could have happened after fulfilling this fantasy I had since last summer. What objective could I try to achieve, now? While the three girls were sleeping I asked myself if it was still snowing and I was hungry too. I went to the kitchen trying to fix something for breakfast. While eating I heard one of the three woke up and she was coming to the kitchen; I was very curious to hear her comments on the night before now that we were sober. Camilla came in wearing the same clothes from the night before. I didn't tell her anything but "Good morning", curious of her first words. She sat down, beside me and started preparing her breakfast taking things here and there. Her hair was a mess and her face proved how much she drank the night before; she looked right in my eyes and smiled. "How did you like it last night?" She asked.

"Oh if I like it…it was incredible" I answered. "Yes, was it the first time with three girls together?" She asked. "Yes. And I hope it won't be the last." I answered making clear I didn't want to consider that as a "one-time" experience. She nodded and I asked "What about you, was this the first time?" "Yes…." She answered smily, looking as she was thinking about a second time. We kept eating till Chiara arrived in the kitchen. She was wearing a pajama that made her look so sexy; she sat down and she looked at us in conspiratorial way. "Do you remember what happened last night?" After a silent moment we cracked down laughing. It was clear she remembered everything and that she liked it too; she started eating with us and she told me that was the first time for her as well. It was obvious, she did it the first time with me just a few days before. Giulia was the only one missing, she was still on the sofa sleeping. I was surprised by the easy atmosphere talking about the night before; it was new for each one of us but no one seemed embarrassed. Even the fact that Giulia and I were "exes" about to starting to date again seemed not to be a problem. We were all relaxed as what happened the night before had been the most natural thing in the world. Actually that was the way it was. "Sex is the most natural thing in the world." I thought. We all expressed what we felt inside; what was not so healthy was constantly keeping inside our feelings worrying to be judged or scared for the consequences. All the limits we had were keeping us far from happiness. What we had done was the deepest expression of our instincts and the great pleasure we lived was the natural consequence. We were talking about it naturally, in an open and easy way. The general mood was high. Giulia finally joined us in the kitchen. I looked at her and said: "Giulia, You look horrible, what did you do last night?" We started laughing hard and she answered: "I think I participate to an orgy but I'm not sure if I was dreaming or not. It seemed real." She looked at her girlfriends and she realized it hadn't been a dream. The girls looked happy and my self-esteem was at the top. "Everything I remember really happened? Giulia asked. "It depends, honey, what do you remember?" I immediately answered and I added "If you really remember everything considering how drunk we were...well it means you enjoyed it a lot..." I told her. She looked at time straight in the eyes and she bit her lips without saying anything as she she did every time she was excited. I knew her very well and I understood her body language perfectly. I started asking myself if what we had done could happen a second time. Maybe soon. I was realizing, in those last weeks, that change and stepping up made me want more. Every time I achieved something I started focusing on the next level believing I could do it. It was a virtuous circle that was taking me in a new dimension. I even thought that new Luke born from the Test was already old. "Luke 3" was here now, motivated and self conscious, years far from myself the way I was a month before. I started asking myself if it was still me or somebody else; I was so far from the past I even thought I changed my "nature". Anyway, this was the "real Luke", and the one before, always insecure and shy, stuck by his limits and fears didn't represented my real potential. Somehow I started living everyday taking the best out of each opportunity. And I felt great.

CHAPTER 22

LOVE YOU KEEP IS PAIN YOU LIVE

After breakfast, we cleaned up the living room throwing away all the beer cans and the bottle of wine we had plus the alcoholic chess glasses. I realized how much we drank. I took a shower. It was still snowing outside with the strong chance to be stuck at Chiara's all afternoon long. Schools were closed with no news yet. I was in the bathroom, the shower open when Giulia came in, took her clothes off making me understand she wanted to take "a shower" with me. Making love in Chiara's bathroom seemed interesting so I took the chance.

I thought it was almost ironic having sex with "just" one girl. Anyway I had the whole day with the three girls and I was ready for anything to happen. Giulia and I left the bathroom satisfied and once downstairs we saw Chiara and Camilla laughing, like as they heard us. After the night before, we had no inhibition and I didn't feel embarrassed. We spent the morning in front of TV and Facebook. As I predicted, the party was postponed because of the bad weather. I chatted with Tiffany and Ilary: they were sorry they didn't see me that night. What if they knew I was together three beautiful girls I spent the night with having "fun". I could had have fun with them too, they were always looking for me, making me feel so desired. While chatting with them, Giulia, Chiara and Camilla started watching their favorite TV series "The vampire diaries". I wasn't looking but from a far view it didn't seem so bad. I asked "Anyone knows what is going on outside?". They didn't even answered, too busy with the tv. I threw Chiara a pillow and she didn't even move. Another one to Giulia starting laughing. I started bombing them with all the pillows I could find trying to get their attention. They turned at me during the break starting a pillow battle. We were battling hard having a lot of fun when the tv series "called" them again, turning in to silence. Well, no problem, I kept on chatting with Tiffany and Ilary who were waiting for me on the chat. They were very different from each other but both very cute. I could have fun with them, I mean, not in a serious relationship, just for pleasant "adventure" moments. Things had being changing a lot lately, big turmoils: the affair with Chiara, then explaining Giulia, feeling back near to her, then the awareness of my strong attraction to Chiara and, last but not least, LAST NIGHT, something incredible and new. I was glad for Giulia's forgive; knowing she had accepted my attraction to Chiara made me feel so good. My fears were just mental limits which never even came true. This told myself again what I started thinking: following the voice inside my soul, instinct in other words, doubts and worries were losing importance. Following the steps for my happiness transmitted me a sense of self-confidence which was freeing me from fear and hesitation, allowing me to achieve the goals I felt inconceivable, feeling self-confident as never before. After all, I've never done anything particular to make what happened the night before real and anyway I realized a very important goal without a proportioned logic effort. I found myself "casually" stuck in a house with three gorgeous girls and events allowed me to reach something I never thought it could be possible. I could never believe in casualty anymore and actually I never did; but now I was sure. Maybe the meaning behind the events wasn't always clear but I knew there was a meaning. Thinking about what happened the night before, even if I promised myself not to analyze each situation anymore, I could think about just one thing: excluding coincidence, I felt I reached the goal simply because I didn't know it was impossible. During the night, I didn't do anything to stop myself from living that experience; I didn't tell myself" I can't" and I didn't listen to limits I imposed myself. I enjoyed the situation from the beginning without thinking about it too much, without thinking I couldn't made my dreams come true. As a consequence, I had the best night in my life. In other words I lived the moment without judging and evaluating the single aspect. I let emotions take me (and he girls did the same) and we lived what we always dreamed of: girls and boys enjoying pure attraction without limits, fears or doubts. The most ancient part of our brain won, the deepest part of our soul, allowing us to live one of the best nights ever. The emotions had been able to express themselves without shame or embarrassment and the most authentic part of all of us had found expression in one of its most natural and authentic way: sex. It was just what I had always sought in the relationship with the girls. While recognizing the importance of verbal communication, I thought, as I had already expressed, that the best and most effective way of communication was the body language that aroused primordial sentiments in us. The night before was exactly what happened: after the use of words, which often masked what they really felt and wanted to actually communicate, had prevailed the attraction that we each felt for the other sex in a communion of pure emotions that had led us to heights of pleasure than ever before. No more misunderstandings and misinterpretations but just a natural way to a perfect union between the sexes; just phenomenal. I had gone far beyond the initial application of the test to arrive at a level that was much higher than the point where I started initially, and when the test was started, the situation was for me, as for the other guys, difficulties in relating with success with girls. Now I was light years ahead, what had happened the night before showed that not only could establish satisfactory relationships with girls, but I was also able to realize what I considered to be my most effective and enjoyable way to relate with each other sex. In conclusion I had reached a level of awareness that I was able to get exactly what I wanted from each report, or nearly so. The goal we set ourselves for phase three of the Test was on hand for me and I was at the same time load to get to the bottom of this "mission". Assuming, however, that there would have been a term since the improvements, by definition, would never come to an end. I kept chatting with Ilary and Tiffany while Giulia, Chiara and Camilla were still hypnotized in front of TV. I realized they didn't answered yet to my question on the weather situation; we could have been covered by snow without knowing. I went to the window and I could see the situation was pretty bad; I couldn't drive my Vespa. I asked Chiara if we had enough food for the day and, incredibly, she answered: "Ahahah, always worried about food, are you worried you're going to die for hunger here?" "Well, the cook should worry about ingredients for his dishes. How can you survive if I don't cook?" I joked. "If you cook, I'll find everything you need!". She said smiling. She had a beautiful face. I started preparing lunch.

Chiara joined me in the kitchen and we started cooking something good. Like the night before, I had a good time. We were preparing sauce when our proximity became really dangerous; attraction towards her was pretty strong and this time I didn't allow my thoughts to stop me. We kissed and it was incredible. That wasn't the first time I kissed her but every time it was better. It was long and intense and unusually I didn't care about Giulia could see us. After all we weren't back together yet but this wasn't the real reason. The reason was that I learned to follow my feelings and this was a lesson I learned from the Test, deeply learned. If I had kept having doubts on my behavior every time, I would have kept making the wrong thing, frustrating what the Test taught me since then. This time with Chiara I had no intention to waste it all. After kissing, we kept cooking as nothing had happened, calling Giulia and Chiara once the lunch was ready. Another little suggestion I was getting from the Test (almost as if it was another entity telling me what to do), was that the same concepts of right and wrong were relative; or rather they were not as definite as I thought and the judgement on each experience considered many more shades. It was something I would have still thought about. We ate good enjoying that particular situation; who would have ever said that we would remain the four of us locked at home because of the snow? I started wondering how we could have spent the afternoon and eventually the evening. Certainly, I didn't excluding the chance to repeat what had happened the night before. After eating we laid on the couch and I don't remember how, a certain discussion about "real love" started. It surely wasn't me to suggest the subject but anyway I found myself in the middle of it. I left room to the three girls that loved discussing about these things while I started chatting on facebook with Old John to keep me updated on the Test evolution. Until Camilla involved me by asking my opinion. I immediately thought I should have weighed carefully what I would say but then I realized that I was thinking too much so I simply said what I thought. "First of all it depends on what you mean by real love. If it's the obvious one we see in movies than we speak about different things. That is simply false representation of a relation between a man and a woman that in reality will be different. The scriptwriters know how to create a story and some characters that will be loved by spectators. But there is nothing real in all this. Really different is love arising in reality which is more genuine and authentic than the one you watch on TV or in the movies. If for some strange reason you think that in real life it doesn't exist I think that this is partially due to the fact that your mind has a distorted idea because of what you saw on TV series where everything is easy and magic and partially is due to the fact that love in everyday life needs courage and desire of opening yourself to the other risking to be hurt. Therefore I wonder: Do you desire to risk in order to really know the other person up to the point to became vulnerable?. Or would you watch TV series dreaming of something that will never happen until you engage yourself with passion in a relation? The right question is "Are you brave enough to believe in love or you give up even before trying?" There was a silent moment as if my answer had confused them and I really think it did. Surely it wasn't the answer they expected even more from male. "I understand what you mean. So you believe that real love can exist?" Camilla said. "I think it depends on us. Love is not an entity in itself. It's a felling which is generated by the union of two people available to forget fear and sorrow in order to fall in each other arms. More courage you've got, better are the chances of experimenting ecstasy coming from real love. But it depends on and exclusively on us. Saying that it doesn't exist means to renouncing and refusing to play the game because you are to coward to live life fully. To cut it short love you keep is pain you live." It was a satisfactory answer and I thought that what I was saying was sharable. I went on: "Surely it is easier to think that real love does not exist and do nothing about it rather than working on it, fearless to understand another person fully. But what's easier is rarely the right thing to do. What is needed to grow is always difficult and complex but always possible. The real wisdom is in facing difficulties as they are to become what we are destined to be. Love for another person is perhaps one of the most difficult things just because makes us feel fragile toward the other and before toward ourselves and maybe what it is hard for us to accept is sometimes our deep nature." I would have liked to have the girls thinking about these topics with more critical spirit and less disillusion. I refused to think so young girls did not believe in love. And more because I've always thought this topic was a prerogative of women, always more careful and mature about feelings than men. They felt just disillusion for past experiences, I thought, more than being really convinced. Maybe what I just had told them could have helped to change their minds or to think deeply before stating not to believe in on of the most important thing in life. Chiara answered: "You know Luke, I didn't expect such an answer. Normally guys are not serious about these subject or anyway they don't show big interest. I liked what you said." Camilla joined her saying: "I like to think what you've said is true. It is even nicer because it came from a guy." I jokingly thought that I was going to to feel moved. I felt that what I had expressed had been really understood and this could have helped to create a much deeper relation with the female sex. This was the point I had "to work "on if I wanted to improve my relationships with girls. We kept on talking exchanging ideas and considerations for a couple of hours and I surely enjoyed it. I had really changed if now I could feel the pleasure of even just talking with girls for hours. It was for me the final trial that would establish if my growth had supplied me with solid foundations for my improvement. And from what I could see, the answer was affirmative. I started understanding that the life I lived was always and first of all a relation with ourselves and if there was something I can't accept, that concerned first of all a part of me. When I looked outside and criticized what I was really doing was criticizing that part of me that the observed thing reflects back. On the other hand, if I focused on the beauty that surrounded us, I could observe first of all what was beautiful inside of me. If in the past I had difficulties in establishing successful relations with girls, the problem was not outside but inside of me. It probably showed my limit of accepting a part of myself. What I had done up to now and I kept doing, was not modifying the outside thing but working on my change, in accepting myself completely. "Only when you are able to accept what you are without any judgement but with total mental opening, acceptance and love, you are able to deal with other people in a significant way". This was the thought I had while we were talking. I shared it with the girls and I think they agreed. I felt that from a certain point of view they needed to be able to believe in what I said. "Actually all of us need to believe in the possibility of being able to reach the highest levels of happiness through the love shared with another person. It's the essence of life. If we state our disillusion on these topics is just because of disappointments and suffering that we experienced in the past, not because we don't believe it. But it's our nature itself that will inevitably let us disclose our deep and rooted desire of relation with the person that shares our path of life. We can't do nothing but accept with courage what we have in front of us." I lingered to think about the afternoon we were spending and how interesting and different it was becoming. This was a challenge too and it was also a way to get to know myself better in the relation with beautiful girls that supplied me with useful cues for reflecting. Since I had solidly acquired the position of cook, around 5 o'clock I started preparing hot chocolate for me and for the three girls. From the window I could see clearly that it was still snowing and a quick view to the "status updates" on Facebook confirmed me that conditions were not good at all. Chiara's parents were still in the house in the mountains and considering weather conditions in town I could not think about the situation at high altitude. Probably they would not be back for a few days. That's ok I thought. It seemed almost that Chiara's house had changed into a micro world where I could live a piece of real life with all its challenges and reflections. Really weird. I realized that none of us had problems in being locked in that situation and I felt that we all were having benefits and a lot of fun. I myself was taking notes of a lot of things on which I could reflect speaking with John. A lot of ideas that could help us and we could have shared with the guys from the school to help them in their growth. Actually, to have become the reference point for the guys from the school was an honor and at the same time it made us determined not to disillude their trust in us. Without considering that this "position" was pushing us to grow more in order to help all the guys better. A virtuous circle that didn't let us to stay there sitting on our asses but that was giving us an incredible courage in facing any situation. Being able to help other human beings to get better was the best reward. "In a certain way when you help somebody to obtain a result impossible for himself, you get the best out of it indirectly in a strong way. Helping the others was giving sense and value to our lives." I thought. The chocolate was ready and I invited Giulia, Chiara and Camilla to have some with me. Their were dressed in their sweat suite and once again I thought how a girl looked more attractive in a t-shirt and jumpers like the ones used for the hip hop dance, more than with an elegant dress. Better to be simple, because if a girl is cute she doesn't need anything particular to get attention. We enjoyed the chocolate and I received the usual compliments for my cooking talent. I had never done anything this difficult but they appreciate it anyway. The weather situation seemed not to get better and it was obvious that we would have spent the rest of day and the night at Chiara's. After eating I went back chatting with John online to tell him my adventure and share my thought on the intense night before and on this afternoon. Things to reflect on were many and various. We had gone from pure physical attraction to a very intimate dialogue on real love. The range of emotions was wide and all this had happened in less than a day. Very interesting and formative. Very useful to allow me to enlarge my views, making at the same time a change, absolutely necessary, that I had welcomed in the last weeks, as able to take me towards high goals I could reach. I chatted with John about this. As soon as he found out that I was locked in with three hot chicks he told him, joking, that he was on his way all speed. He told me he was engaging himself for the objective that we have stated for part 3 of the Test and he was obtaining results. We decided to post these considerations in the Test group on FB in order to start a discussion that could have been useful for guys form the school. We had seriously accepted our role and we really wanted to help them in that sense. This phase of the Test would have probably been the deepest and most intimate since by trying to get to know the girls better, we would have understood deeper ourselves which it would have been difficult but potentially very useful. I think that these aspects had been understood by the guys and this meant that the effort we were making was going in the right direction. While chatting, Giulia asked me to follow her upstairs. I left my iPad on the table and followed her with curiosity. I understood quickly that she just wanted some intimacy that I didn't deny. After all I desired to stay alone with her too and I missed her company deeply. She had incredible lips that I loved kissing and biting and a perfume that brought back to my mind the wonderful moments spent together. My relation with her, even with the new developments, was really special and unique. No other girl made me feel the way I did when I was with her and this proved clearly why Giulia was my unique girlfriend. We weren't back together officially and recent events had confused the picture a little bit more; nevertheless I had no doubts about my feeling for her. It was the same for her, I think. I was really grateful I found a girl so sweet and special who understood me right away, accepting me the way I was without judging and able to forgive my recents "mistakes". The right adjective was "unique".

I told her because it was important to recognize her value opening myself to her and, at he same time, letting her know what I felt for her, deeply inside. Rarely in the past I showed my self vulnerable as I had been to her and this had probably been my limit: I wanted to be different now and I told her clearly what I was feeling. I realized I could have had fun with Chiara, Camilla, Ilary or Tiffany but Giulia remained the best for me. "You know giulia, I want to tell you something..." We were lying on Chiara's bed, hugging each other and she was watching me with her big blue eyes and her beautiful face. "You are really unique to me, I feel that when I am with you there is no other girl in the world who can make me feel the same. I'd like to tell you that you have a special place in my heart." She was almost crying. Then she kissed me and said: "You know Luke despite these last events I found the strength to forgive you because I feel you are the right guy for me and I can't see me with nobody else." We kept kissing with intensity and passion. All of a sudden Chiara came in not remembering that we were there; she smiled at us apologizing.

After what happened the night before we could not feel embarrassed. Giulia and I went back downstairs in the living room and I felt in that moment our relation was really strong and solid. At the same time I felt that other experiences like the one of the night before could happen again without damaging my relation with Giulia. This did not have much sense from a logical point of you but I learnt that pure rationality did not mean too much in my life. Giulia herself did not seem to have many problems talking about what happened the night before or about my attraction for Chiara. It was clear that girls think in a different way from the guys, but anyway I did not understand too much. Wild instinct was guiding my life and everything happening to me was above simple comprehension; I just had to act listening to the voice inside me, living my desires and expressing my emotions. This was it. In doing this I could neither ask myself too many questions nor have negative thoughts as fears, embarrassment or anything else. From my point of view, this was kind of crazy but I was experimenting it and the results were there. I could enjoy my relation with Giulia but, at the same time, I could have fun with other chicks and everything seemed to work perfectly. I did not want to ask myself why it shouldn't. I just had to live all situation in a great way, without any judgement and with total mental opening and acceptance for whatever was happening to me. I started understanding that things didn't happen casually but it was myself that lead events always in the right direction. Finally I was the master of my life. The situations that one day I had just dreamed were finally a reality and they were giving me the chance to enjoy life in all its greatness. My thoughts were interrupted by Camilla who had just a shower and was coming out of the bathroom almost naked; I felt like laughing because lately there was always this balance between my deep philosophical meditations and naked girls crossing my life and enriching it of pleasure. The way of reflecting of old Luke was still there but in a new proactive way towards concrete goals. Camilla wearing just a towel was sensual and irresistible. While she came out I went in looking for my iPhone. I thought I could have left it there after the "shower" I had with Giulia a few hours earlier. While I was looking for it I heard the door shutting, I turned and saw Chiara naked starring at me. I couldn't speak for a few seconds, then she started getting closer. My heart was beating faster. Attraction was very strong and hardly could I resist. After all, why should I? She put the towel down near me showing herself in her complete beauty. Then she turned and came inside the shower without saying anything. I was a little perplexed, I thought she would try to kiss me: I waited for my physical contact but nothing happened. I left the bathroom and then I realized that she could have just provoked me in order to invite me to have a shower with her. "What a fool!" I said to myself.

To verify this I went back into the bathroom, took off my clothes and got into the shower without saying anything. In the beginning it seemed I was wrong but immediately after, she confirmed what I thought. We let ourselves go with passion showing the attraction that dominated us. We just kissed not going further and I felt this was all wanted in that moment. Again, no logics. I dressed and went back to the living room sitting close to Giulia, watching some music videos on tv. I could still see images of what I had just done with Chiara and really I had a hard time to understand if what I was doing was right or wrong. In spite of my promises of abandoning a logic view, I could not avoid meditating every time I lived situations apparently senseless. In this case I was justifying myself thinking that until Giulia didn't care, why should I. This gave me a minimum of tranquility even if it didn't help me to clear up my ideas. I decided to stop thinking waiting for new hints to reflect on. I had already told myself many times I had to stop analyzing always each situation in all the deepest details but I still fell in to the same mistake. How could Giulia not be worried for my attraction for Chiara? But, it was true enough that after the night before it was really useless to keep asking questions. It was so impossible to understand that maybe it was just the case of unplugging the brain. I kept hugged to Giulia for a while until Camilla joined us on the couch. Then I heard Chiara screaming to reach her outside in the yard. I went out and saw she was pointing my poor Vespa completely covered with snow. We had been stuck in the house for all that time without realizing how much snow had piled up. The roads were not clean so I definitely knew that I had to spend the night at Chiara's. Considering the happenings of the night before I was happy about it. Moreover I started wondering about the chances that it could happen again. Chiara started trowing me snowing balls and so just joking we ended lying in the snow. I don't think it was by chance because she started immediately to hug me trying to kiss me. I enjoyed the moment extremely amusing. We rolled in the snow like kids laughing like crazy. I realized how little we need to be really happy...

CHAPTER 23

IT'S OUR GREATNESS THAT SCARES US

Even if the pure and wild instinct was holding the reins of my life, the constant reflecting kept staying inside of me for my extremely reflective nature. Until this continuous meditating was not an obstacle or rather it fitted perfectly in the optics of the "new Luke", I was happy to maintain this feature. Actually I found it useful to be able to connect with myself at a deeper and more intimate level, helping to make the right choices. I was sunk in the snow with Chiara on me laughing as crazy: that moment generated a sensation in me that I had never felt before. It was as if time had stopped, as if nothing else existed but the two of us. We were perfectly living the present without brooding over the past or dreaming on the future: it was the essence of the "carpe diem" that we had recently studied at school on which I had meditated a lot. I found weird not to have felt before that completely new sensation. After all in the last period I had spent some moments far more intense with Giulia or Chiara. Therefore, how only now I felt in me that feeling so deep that connected me so powerfully with the present moment? It was evident that, even if I had lived more intense moments in the last weeks, only now I was really ready to make a further step towards totally new emotions that I had never experimented before. My wild way of growing that in the last times had catapulted me in unreal situations, was now taking me towards tops of pleasure that I didn't even think possible.

At this point, without any doubt, it was clear that even the word itself "limit" had no sense. I tried my best in the mental effort of abandoning definitively all form of limit, fear, judgment and all those negative emotions that systematically prevented me from tasting life up to the core. In the last weeks the steps had been big but I felt that it was just the beginning of something I couldn't see the end of. Because there was no end. In one of these philosophical moments fed by the presence of a beautiful girl, it came to my mind Kierkegaard thought that I had recently read: "Nothing scares the man more than the conscience of the immensity of what he is able to do or become." Without presumption I think that this was exactly the new consciousness I had reached in that moment. And this literally unsettled me. I think that, as for everybody, my fears had always been failing, being hurt or relative to something that could in some way hurt you. This was was normal but now all was changing. What really scares the man is not really something negative but his own greatness! The asleep potentialities, not yet expressed are really what scares the man! "If we realized everything that we are able to, becoming all that we can become, we would be literally shocked!" I think this was another quotation but I couldn't remember the source. There was a further turning point for me. In the last times the change was so quick that surprises were continuous. This one was so strong that it took me a while before absorbing it. The fact itself of accepting that it was our greatness to scare us, and not something negative, was shocking and at the same time terribly exciting. I felt shivers of pleasure down my back and I clearly knew it was not due to the snow. Useless to say that a new phase had already started for me. I didn't know myself at this point where I could have got to. The pure mystery of infinitely grand things that were reaching me, was charging me of such a powerful energy that I was literally flying. I was open to trust that the best, as always, was still to come. I mentally thanked Chiara for having inspired this shocking awareness. Nothing would have been the same. We went back home where Giulia and Camilla had been wondering where we had been. If only the three of them had known what was going in my mind. I smiled and sat on the couch, close to Giulietta that was smelling like a rose. I put my mind in stand by and enjoyed some cuddles. These radical changes in my believes were bursting my brain and I needed to alternate deep philosophical thoughts with beautiful girls in a balance that was weird but that worked perfectly. After the last revelation I felt much more relaxed and light inside. Giulia knew how to be very sweet and I appreciated so much to stay with her, even just on the couch, relaxing. Her big blue eyes were the thing I loved the most in her. Incredible that I could appreciate the eyes of a girl even before other body parts. It wasn't so obvious. I loved also the smell of her hair and over all I loved to mess up her hair just to joke and have fun. In the meanwhile even Chiara had come in and had sat on the armchair close to us. We were just relaxing and didn't really care about snowing outside and cut off by the snow. It was just a little adventure and it almost seemed that we all had been waiting for it for a while, just like the first time that I had spoken of the Test and we all had shown to have felt that need for months. "It's incredible to see how sometimes, even if several people share a common need, it takes time and special situations to get to a point where everybody can get benefit from a change of the course." I thought. In the beginning of the Test it was my intuition to show the new way, in this case it was the snow. The result was that, thanks to an 'unexpected' event, now the four of us had the chance of living a unique experience that was enriching us at all levels. Therefore not only pure enjoyment but also a lot of useful ideas to improve one selves and grow as human beings. In that moment I thought about my feeling for those girls which was above the simple attraction. Giulia was my unique favorite one, nevertheless I couldn't state that my feelings for Chiara and Camilla were just physical attraction. It was evident that after the last experiences something stronger had established, something that had made me get closer to these wonderful girls. If the Test had started as the answer to a question and had helped us at the same time in our relation with girls, it couldn't be considered but a spectacular success that had led me to such a radical change that I hardly recognized myself. As I had already analyzed it, I couldn't but feel that everything happened up to now was only the beginning of something bigger that was to arrive, overwhelming me. I was really ready to let myself go totally, without fear, since only in this way I could keep getting more satisfactions in a trend so positive that didn't seem real. Therefore I realized that this was just a starting point and I felt like smiling to think how much I had improved up to now and which scenery I had in front of me. The questions were many and the answers could arrive only if I had kept on daring with constance and decision. I also started to understand that if for any reason I had stopped to keep on my new mentality, I wouldn't have got any more improvement and little by little I I would have gone back, in terms of personal growth. It was not possible to remain still. Either I was improving or in the long term I would have gone back. It was like being on a tapis roulant: you needed to walk even just to stand and if you by any chance stopped, you fell violently backwards.

I don't think there was the risk of going back or stopping considering the results that I was getting and the charge that pushed me to go ahead. I was on all speed and nothing and nobody could stop me. These considerations were helped by the physical closeness of Giulia that was hugging my head delicately making me relax and feel in paradise.

CHAPTER 24

WAS EVERYTHING REAL?

At a certain point I thought I went to sleep and when I woke up I was shocked to see around me a completely different reality: I was in my room, on my bed and not at Chiara's. It took me a while to realize what was going on: I couldn't figure out what of the two was the dream. I felt a bad sensation through my body, almost as if what I had lived up to now was nothing but a dream. I looked around and started understanding that this was the reality and I felt terrible. How was it possible that all the experiences I went through in the last month were just a fantasy generated by my mind while sleeping? Was everything false? Was I different or was I the same I was before? It looked like an unreal situation. I got up from my bed to try to clear up my ideas...pretty dangerous attempt. If I had got to the conclusion that what I went through was just a dream, I would have felt even worse. It was really too odd: the whole period of the events seemed to me to have lasted at least a month, too long of a period to be contained within a dream. What was happening? Nothing of what I had seen and lived had really happened? I was going to go crazy. I got my iPhone and found a message from Giulia from September 14. Which was yesterday. Apparently we were boyfriend and girlfriend and there was no trace of Tiffany or Ilary. The same messages from Chiara dated the beginning of September, before I started dating Giulia. It seemed as if time had stopped. Or rather that I had lived the impression of living a whole month of adventures and growth while actually it was just a dream. I remember that in my dream the 15 of September was the day when John, in the evening, had invited me to a pub to let me talk for the first time about the Test. I started having shivers along my back for the thought that I might have anticipated all the future events in my dream. I decided to go back to sleep to see if I really had a premonition. I went to sleep fast and all of a sudden I found myself in Chiara's house with Giulia hugging my Head and Camilla sitting near us. "Oh, my God...", I thought. It was too real to be a dream. Now after seeing the other reality, I started having thousand of doubts about which of the two situations was a dream. Just a little before I thought I had woken up but now I started to be confused and not to understand what was going on. I heard a strange sound similar to my clock and in no time I found myself in my bed, in my house. Maybe this was the reality and all the great experiences lived were just a dream even if incredibly beautiful. I went to school thinking of the situation and the whole day I did nothing but meditate. In the afternoon Giulia came to my house, just like in the dream. I didn't know if I was still the old Luke, locked up by his fears and thousand limits or if I was changed for real. That night when John came to my place, I understood that what I had lived in the dream or whatever that was, had been a premonition of my imminent future. I heard also the same words.

"Luke! Luke, come and see!" I felt very weird sensations half way between pure curiosity and excitement because I knew what was going to happen to me.

Had I really foreseen the future? Which implications would this have had in my life? If I had already foreseen everything, could I also have changed the course of events anticipating what would happen? But what would this have determined? Actually I didn't know yet that that night would have been incredibly different from what I had expected. My life wouldn't have been the same anymore...

DO YOU LIKE TO KNOW THE WAY THE STORY IS GOING TO CONTINUE?

FIND MORE INFO ON MY SITE:

www.LucaGrisendiArt.com

on my facebook page:

www.facebook.com/lucagrisendiart

and on Youtube:

www.Youtube.com/LucaGrisendiArt

The best is yet to come...